Freedom from Allergy Cookbook

Ronald Greenberg MD
Angela Nori

Revised Expanded Edition

Blue Poppy Press

Note to readers:
The information in this book is for educational purposes only. It is not intended, and should not be considered, as a replacement for consultation, diagnosis or treatment by a duly licensed health practitioner.

Cover design: DesignGeist
Cover painting: Lemon Tea by Chloe Greenberg
Printed in Canada

Canadian Cataloguing in Publication Data

Greenberg, Ron, 1949-
    Freedom from allergy cookbook

    Includes index.
    First ed. published under title: So what can I eat, eh?
    ISBN 0-9680302-0-3

    1. Food allergy - Diet therapy - Recipes   I. Nori, Angela,
    II. Title III. Title: So whatcan I eat, eh:
    RC588.D53G74 1995   641.5'631   C95-911187-5

Blue Poppy Press
212-2678 West Broadway
Vancouver, B.C. Canada V6K 2G3

Table of Contents

Introduction

If you have just discovered that you have food allergies, relax. It is likely that over the next months you will be able to reintroduce many of the foods you are avoiding. You will be better able to deal with the current necessary dietary changes if you are optimistic, calm and well prepared. You are avoiding food allergens to rest your immune system. It is helpful also to rest your mind. Instead of maintaining a sense of deprivation, you could develop a positive sense of helping yourself to greater health by staying away from things that adversely affect you. By changing the foods that you eat, you are bringing out your basic healthiness that is being obscured by what you have unknowingly been doing to yourself. Be flexible, let yourself acquire a taste for new foods and new patterns of choosing foods.

Because both of the authors are busy and like to eat we developed these recipes so that you can prepare them with a minimum of fuss and time. We know that people with allergies get hungry too. You may notice that the recipes are low in salt and fat. They are also suitable for people trying to lower their cholesterol level. You will be introduced to many delicious foods that you might otherwise never discover.

The recipes are divided into four separate days using different ingredients each day to give you a wide range of foods to choose from. Before you use the recipes in this book, stop! You will find that cooking and eating a wide variety of foods will be much easier if you first read the sections before the recipes.

In this new updated and expanded edition of Freedom From Allergy Cookbook we have doubled the number of recipes and reorganized them to give you easier access to even more options of things to eat.

Allergy in an adult or child can create difficult or painful symptoms. But you can control and overcome allergies. Many of us feel helpless when we or our children are ill. We wish that there was something more that we could be doing. This feeling of helplessness can stop us from actively taking part in helping ourselves to find the way back to health. This book will help you and your family take a more active role in controlling allergy.

Your change of diet may pose many new options. Beyond the question of "What can I eat?" is the question, "How do I prepare it?" This book is designed for people who know or suspect that they are sensitive to one or more foods and wish to avoid them. You will find information on what foods to avoid, what foods to substitute and how to prepare them quickly and easily. No complicated recipes. After reading and using this book, you can be well nourished, eat happily and enjoy foods that enhance your health and well being.

Children with allergies present unique difficulties and opportunities. When illness is caused by allergy to food, parents are often faced with removing a favourite food from their child's diet and seemingly to deprive him of enjoyment. But these changes need not be viewed in a negative light. Parents make these changes expecting that their children will feel better and be happier. But sometimes it is hard to see beyond the initial difficulties that change presents. These initial difficulties could be viewed as opportunities. The changes that the treatment of allergy requires can open a wide range of choices and possibilities that we might otherwise have never seen. For example, most people eat only two dozen different foods out of the hundreds of foods easily available to us. Our distant ancestors foraged for their food and were aware of the variety of foods available at different times of the year and in different places. Unlike them most of us have become accustomed to eating a few foods that are available all year. As a result we have become stereotyped in our eating habits. One result of that may be the development of specific food allergies. Making a child's or adult's food choices more diverse will create new food possibilities for the whole family.

Understanding Allergy

What is an allergy?

An allergy is a negative response to a substance, e.g. dust, pollen or food, that normally would not cause a problem in a non-allergic individual. These reactive substances are called allergens. Allergic reactions occur when an allergen contacts the white blood cells and biochemicals that make up the immune system. Reactions to foods from over eating are not allergies. Reactions caused by digestive problems or food-poisoning are not allergies. Sometimes it is difficult to distinguish a true allergic reaction from a problem caused by a different mechanism because the resulting symptoms may be the same.

The immune system mechanisms that result in allergy symptoms are in many ways similar to the ways that our bodies control infections. Our immune system is stimulated by infection to reproduce and to produce certain types of cells and biochemicals to kill bacteria and viruses. Similarly, the presence of foods to which we may be allergic causes certain white blood cells called lymphocytes, to release certain proteins called immunoglobulins or antibodies. These immunoglobulins react with other cells in the tissues of our nose, lungs, skin or gut to release biochemicals such as histamine. It is these biochemicals, when they interact with any of our body systems, that initiate the symptoms that we call allergic reactions.

History of allergy

The ancient Greeks knew some of the problems created by allergy. The 2000 year old Hebrew Talmud records allergy symptoms. Records of abnormal reactions to drugs exist from the time of the famous and influential physician Galen of the second century. It was in the early nineteenth century that a French physiologist first described severe reactions in animals injected repeatedly with proteins. This was the first experimentally created allergic reaction. In 1906 Drs. Clemens Von Pirquet and Bella Schick introduced the word allergy. They derived it from the Greek phrase "*allos ergos*" which means altered reactivity. The word allergy refers to negative reactions from exposure to normally harmless materials. It was also in 1906 that hayfever was first recognised to be the result of an altered immune system response. Four years later asthma was recognized to have an immunological basis. In 1919, physicians first developed experimental desensitization (allergy shots) of allergens. About the same time skin testing for allergens was introduced. In the early thirties physicians developed the elimination diet approach to diagnosing food allergy. But it was not until the mid-sixties that Immunoglobulin E (IgE), the immunoglobulin (antibody) responsible for immediate type allergic reactions, was purified. This was an important step in discovering the interactions of white blood cells that control the allergic response.

Why do I have allergies?

If you are allergic to anything, you probably inherited the predisposition to allergy from your parents. If both of your parents have allergies, then you have at least a 75% chance of developing allergies some time in your life. With one allergic parent there is a 40% probability. Many people only realize that they have a family history of allergy after they discover their own allergy and start checking other family members. Often allergies will appear, relatively late in life, to substances that apparently had been well tolerated for years. However, if you think back you may be able to trace the subtle effects allergies have had in your life for many years.

The particular foods to which you become allergic depend on what exposures you have had. For example, North Americans are frequently reactive to milk and wheat while Asians eating traditional foods are often reactive to rice and soy bean. Sometimes the development of allergy follows an infection. Sometimes it seems to follow exposure to chemicals. It is the repeated use of specific foods that determines to which foods you will probably become allergic. Recent studies indicate that the number of people with allergies and their severity is increasing and that chemical pollution of our air, food and water may play a role in the development of allergies. Generally, urban populations have more problems than rural.

Any food or food additive can be allergenic. The most common food allergens in the Western diet are: milk, wheat, yeast, corn, citrus, egg, soy, peanut, shellfish and chocolate.

How is food allergy different?

In order to control your allergies, it is useful to understand the nature of food allergy. Food allergies can appear in two different ways; either as fixed or as cyclical reactions. Cyclical food allergies can appear as either masked or unmasked reactions. Allergies to airborne inhalants such as dust mite, pollens or animal danders are similar to fixed food allergies.

1. Fixed food allergy

Fixed food allergies are the type of reactions that some people have every time that they eat or even breathe the fumes of a small amount of a particular food. Often these reactions are strong and potentially dangerous. They appear soon after contact with the food. This type of allergic reaction is a lifelong pattern and is unlikely to disappear. Most people have no problem identifying a fixed food allergy reaction. Fixed food allergens will always need to be avoided. People with a fixed food reaction to a fish should be cautious with all fish. Similarly, be cautious with all nuts and seeds if you are very reactive to one.

2. Cyclical food allergy - Why do food allergies seem to come and go?

Cyclical food reactions follow a different pattern. If you have this type of allergic response you may notice a reaction but not each time you eat the food. Your reactions may range from being quite weak to being more severe, but are seldom dangerous. In fact, many times you may not notice your reaction at all. When noticed, the reaction may take place many hours after you ate the food. The presence and strength of a cyclical food allergy depends on how much you eat and how often you eat a particular food. For example, drinking one glass of milk once a week may not cause you any noticeable reaction. However, drinking two or three glasses at once (increased amount) or drinking one glass two or three days in a row (increased frequency) may result in a noticeable allergic reaction, either soon after or many hours after drinking the milk. With constant exposure to an allergy, acute symptoms may temporarily disappear or become chronic as your body tries to adapt to the exposure.

3. Food addiction - Why is it always my favourite foods?

If a reaction occurs soon after eating a food and you can attribute it to the food, that is called an unmasked reaction. If the reaction occurs many hours after eating the food or if it is very mild and you do not make the connection, the reaction is said to be masked. Masked cyclical reactions are probably the most common type. They are the reason many people do not realize that their health problems are related to foods. Repeated use of a food to which you are reacting can result in symptoms that become chronic and do not necessarily occur or worsen at the time that you eat the food. Because some people feel slightly stimulated - frequently without noticing it - after eating a reactive food and let down hours later, they may come to crave the food that is giving them delayed adverse symptoms. Some people may also feel poorly for a couple of days when they avoid a reactive food. As a result, they may think they need the food to stay healthy, although it is more likely to be the source of their health problems. These stimulatory and withdrawal patterns have led to the use of the phrase, "food addiction" to describe this pattern of food reactivity. These patterns can lead to craving, and over-eating or over-drinking specific foods. Often we may think that a food that we crave is good for us. Obviously this is not true for people who crave salt, sugar, coffee, alcohol and tobacco. Indeed, it is frequently the foods that we crave that cause many of our reactions. Simply giving up these foods for a few weeks can often have a remarkably beneficial effect.

4. Unmasking food allergy

To unmask a food allergy it is necessary to completely avoid the suspected food for four or five days. This includes hidden sources of the food in prepared or restaurant meals. Eating the food may then result in a noticeable and unexpected reaction. The nature of cyclical food allergy is such that if you avoid the allergen for a sufficiently long period, your reaction to the food may disappear. This is one reason not to despair if you are allergic to your favourite food. If you are patient, you will probably be able to eat that food again without reacting to it.

Working With Your Allergies

What can I do about my allergies?

There are only a few ways to solve the problems caused by food allergies. Allergy shots, called immunotherapy by physicians, often work very well for airborne inhalant allergies such as pollens. However, they have not worked as reliably for food allergies. More recently a newer, more effective, method of food desensitization called enzyme potentiated desensitization has been developed in England. There are occasionally people who have various endocrine (hormonal) or other problems who find that their allergies improve when these problems are corrected. Sometimes the use of adequate amounts and appropriate types of nutritional supplements can be of benefit. It is of great value to stop smoking since smoking increases the number and severity of allergies and infections. Controlling any allergies to inhalant allergens by avoidance or immunotherapy can sometimes increase your overall tolerance for reactive foods. Reducing the amount of stress in your life can also help a great deal. Frequently, allergies become much worse when people are under emotional stress from jobs or relationships, and then improve when the stress is reduced. This is probably the reason some people, including some doctors, will tell you that allergies are all in your head. Reducing stress through regular moderate exercise, relaxation techniques or meditation can be of enormous value. Minimizing exposure to bothersome chemicals such as perfume, tobacco, exhaust fumes and plastic smells may be useful.

However, probably the most important thing that you can do to control your allergy symptoms is to avoid the allergenic foods that you have been eating. The rest of this book has been written to help you to do just that.

What is a Rotation Plan?

The Rotation Plan (see page 60) is a pattern for eating a wide range of different foods, organized so that you do not keep eating the same foods day after day. The Rotation Plan has several important advantages for you. First, when you start avoiding a reactive food, you may be tempted to replace it with just one other food. As a result of the repeated use of this other food, you may become reactive to it as well. Similarly, after avoiding the reactive food for several months, you may stop reacting to it but if you start eating it every day again, you may once more become sensitive to it. Second, you probably have not been allergy tested for every food that you eat. Rotation can help control reactions from these untested foods.

You may also have discovered that some foods give you only minor problems when you eat them, especially if you eat them infrequently. You can prevent further problems from arising and perhaps control present minor problems by rotating your foods. This means that any food will be eaten only once in four days and avoided for the next three days. Occasionally, people find that they are only sensitive to one category of food such as meats or grains or fruits. In this situation, it may be necessary to only rotate that one category. It is usually helpful to rotate the grain group. The Rotation Plan can also be used to develop alternatives to specific foods you need to avoid. Look across the columns for ideas for alternatives in each category.

There are two ways to eat using the Rotation Plan. You can start each day of rotation with breakfast and eat the allowed foods on that day until you go to bed. Alternatively, you could start the rotation day with your evening meal and continue it until lunch or coffee break the next afternoon. This would allow you to use supper leftovers for breakfast or lunch.

The numbers beside the food names on the Rotation Plan page refer to the biological family to which the food belongs. All foods with the same number, e.g. soy and peanut - 14, belong to the same family and should always be eaten on the same day. You may find it more convenient to eat a certain food on a different day than the one to which it is assigned. In that case you should move all the foods with the same number to that new day. You may eat as many of the foods from a given day, from any of the categories that you wish, except the foods to which you are sensitive. If you wish to eat a food from another rotation day, it will not cause a problem if you have not eaten it for at least the previous 3 days and avoid it for at least the next 3 days. Some people feel better if they eat a food only once in the day. To others this does not matter. This rotation plan was arbitrarily created with a view to providing foods from all the food categories on each day. Eventually you may want to create your own rotation pattern based on your food preferences. Sometimes foods within a family are cross-reactive. For example, if you are sensitive to tomato, you may also react to green pepper and eggplant. While you do not need to avoid all the foods in a family, if you are reactive to one member of a family, you should be watchful for any reactions from eating other members of the family. Most people who react to wheat also react to rye, spelt, kamut and barley; they should also be avoided. Yogurt, cheese and ice cream almost always will be cross-reactive foods if you are milk sensitive. Most people, 70% or more, who react to cow's milk will also react to goat's milk. It too should be avoided initially. Other foods that often cross-react are celery and carrot, celery and apple, carrot and apple, all forms of poultry, all members of the cabbage/broccoli family. Less commonly soy and peanut, tomato and green pepper, apple and pear, melon and cucumber, milk and beef may cross react. Occasionally people reactive to wheat will react also to all of the grains including rye, spelt, kamut, barley, oat, rice, wild rice, cane sugar, bamboo shoots, millet and corn. Orange and other citrus fruit cross-react. Pineapple and tomato are not citrus fruits.

What will happen when I go on my avoidance plan?

When you start your avoidance plan, it is important that you carefully avoid all of the foods that your doctor has advised or you suspect, for an initial period of one to three months as he or she has indicated. Check the lists below of wheat, milk, yeast, corn, egg and soy containing foods for disguised names that may appear on labels. The goal of this initial stage is to see how much better you can feel when your sensitivities are well controlled. During the first few days of this period a very small number of people may experience withdrawal reactions from their reactive foods. These are often minor, but foods like coffee and tea can produce stronger withdrawal reactions such as severe headache. You should consult your doctor if the reactions are too unpleasant. When you begin to avoid specific foods it may take just a day or two, or up to two or three months before you start to feel better. If after four to six weeks there has been no improvement and you have been carefully following your avoidance programme, you should see your doctor for reappraisal.

The length of time that you can expect to avoid your specific foods allergens is variable. Fixed food allergens will probably have to be avoided forever. When you are feeling well, your doctor may ask you to challenge your cyclical food allergens one by one to see if you have developed tolerance to any of them. You may find that after several weeks or months you may become tolerant to most or all of these foods. If you decide to eat these tolerated foods again you should rotate them or you may find that eventually you will again start to react to them and feel ill. You may mistakenly assume that your food allergies are gone forever after a period of avoidance and reintroduction of those foods. However, if your old problems return, remember that it might be your food sensitivities becoming active again, particularly if you have not been rotating.

What other dietary changes will I need to make?

While you are exploring your new way of eating, you should also be careful about several other non-specific factors. Many people are allergic to sugar, coffee and tea. These substances can also cause problems, by non-allergic mechanisms, through their metabolic effects on your body. Even though you may not have been allergy tested for them, they should be avoided when you start your new eating pattern.

Alcohol causes problems for many people. It contains allergens such as grains and yeast. By affecting your bowel lining it can also speed the absorption of food allergens and result in faster, more severe reactions to any food allergens. It too can cause non-allergic, metabolic problems. It is best to avoid alcohol.

As mentioned before, smoking can increase the severity and number of your allergies. It should also be completely stopped. Some people are reactive to food additives. The worst of these are food colouring such as tartrazine, food flavouring, MSG and sulphur dioxide. They may seem to be in all foods, but if you read labels carefully and prepare as many foods as possible yourself, you will find avoidance to be much less difficult.

When you shop, read labels carefully. You will find many surprises. You may find having a small freezer very helpful for keeping enough different foods available. Freezing your own fruits, berries, etc. gives you complete control of their content and can save you a lot of money. You can also freeze fish, meats, muffins or vegetables.

How can I eat out while avoiding my allergens?
1. Friends

If you have been invited out for a meal, you could call before and mention your sensitivities and tactfully offer some simple ideas for a tolerated meal such as a meat or fish simply cooked or a salad with the dressing left on the table for the guests to add their own. You could also offer to bring one or two things, that you can tolerate, to complement your friend's meal. If alcohol is being served, ask for mineral water or club soda. If you have not made any advance arrangements you could tell your friends when you arrive that you have specific food allergies and ask that they not be offended if you do not eat certain things.

2. Restaurants

Salad bars or buffet restaurants allow you to see what they have before you serve yourself but ask about hidden ingredients. Always ask if what you have ordered from a menu contains foods to which you are allergic. If, when the food arrives, it contains something that you did not expect, you would be completely justified in sending it back, especially if you could not separate the offending item from the rest of your meal. It often helps if you over-emphasize to the waiter the horrible things that will happen in the restaurant if he or she misleads you.

3. Lunch

The recipes contain many ideas for lunch. Many things that you normally eat for lunch or dinner can be adapted to suit your sensitivities. If you usually take sandwiches with you, place an increased amount of the filling into a container. Perhaps make it into a salad and eat that omitting the bread and substitute with an appropriate muffin, leftover pancake or unyeasted bread from the recipes. Use dinner leftovers in the same way. You could take rice cakes, tortillas or oatcakes which are available at supermarkets or health food stores. It is helpful to make several types of muffins in advance and keep them frozen until you need them. Tag foods in your freezer with coloured labels to distinguish the rotation diet days. Children at school might be given extra muffins, etc. so that they can share their unique meals with their friends without needing to trade for allergenic foods.

Can I cheat on my avoidance?

During the initial period of avoidance of your allergic foods you should not eat any of those foods, otherwise you may not derive any benefit from the avoidance period.

Later, if you must eat any of these foods you could choose just one day in the week for all of your indulgences. That way if you react you will feel poorly for only a day or so. If you lapse a little every day you may find yourself feeling poorly most days of the week since reactions can last for several days.

How to Use the Recipes

You will find in the recipes ideas on how to cook and eat regardless of your sensitivities. All recipes avoid wheat, yeast and milk, but some do not follow the rotation pattern. When using the recipes you will notice that many items are listed as optional. For example, you may see egg, sweetener or a milk alternative in the recipes. Often you can just leave them out, if you are sensitive, correcting for the liquid by adding water. Alternatively, you could check the lists of egg replacers, sugar alternatives or dairy alternatives listed in the following pages. Use one that you can tolerate and that seems appropriate to the recipe. Some recipes will give you suggestions for alternatives. If you are sensitive to a major ingredient in a recipe, you can try to find an alternative for it. Not all alternatives are appropriate in all recipes and some may require the slight modification of liquid or other factors in a recipe. If you are not sensitive to eggs or milk you may add these to some recipes to change their taste or texture. Salt and sweeteners are optional in all recipes and may be omitted. The taste for salt is learned and quickly disappears when not used for a few weeks. Recent research indicates that asthma may be improved by avoiding salt.

The quality of many flours used in these recipes will vary between manufacturers. Storage will also alter them. Therefore, when adding liquid in a recipe you may have to be flexible to achieve a proper batter consistency. Some flours go rancid easily. It is probably best to store small amounts in your refrigerator or freezer.

Testing for Food Allergy

There are many different types of allergy tests being used. None are perfect. Some are better, some are very unreliable. There are many commonly used allergy tests with low or unknown reliability. Ask your doctor about the reliability for food allergy detection of the type of test that is proposed. The most reliable approach is to combine the results of skin testing, which probably gives a slight over-reading of your allergies with a food avoidance and challenge procedure. If there is no one near your home using a reliable test procedure then try testing yourself with the following technique.

Stay completely away from a suspected food for five days. Watch for hidden amounts in prepared food. On the 6th day for lunch or dinner, 3 to 4 hours after your last meal, eat only the food to be tested. Pick a day on which you feel well and stable. Then eat a small portion of that food to see if the challenge reproduces your symptoms. **Do not challenge a food to which**

you have had a strong or fixed food allergy. For example, eat a piece of fruit, or a serving of vegetable. Eat nothing else at that meal. If you are testing wheat, use cracked wheat cereal, cream of wheat or a cracker made with only wheat and water. Do not eat anything else for the next four hours. If you are sensitive to the food tested you will probably react within an hour. But the reaction may occur 4 to 24 hours later. Any change from the way you were feeling before you ate the test food may be a positive reaction. Record in writing how you were feeling before and at 1/2 hourly intervals after eating. If there is no reaction within 24 hours have the same food again. If you are unsure if you reacted avoid the food for five more days and test again.

If you react to the tested food, stay away from it for three to six months and try again. Then if you do not react, that would indicate that you have a cyclical food allergy to that item and the allergy has disappeared. In the future eat that food on rotation (see page 7).

Of course you can always look at the overall pattern of your usual diet and avoid the most common food allergens, i.e. use an elimination diet. What you eliminate depends on where you live and therefore what you eat. In North America the foods to initially avoid would be wheat, milk, yeast, apple, orange, onion, coffee and corn. In the U.S. corn is a very, very frequent allergen. You could also avoid any food you eat more than two times weekly. If you feel better after two to three weeks then try to challenge them one at a time and see if there is a reaction. Of course the precaution above still applies:, do not challenge a food to which you have had a strong or fixed food reaction.

An elimination diet frequently used by physicians would avoid the following:
Milk: all milk containing foods including yogurt and cheese.
Egg: all egg containing foods.
Meat: bacon, sausage, ham, hot dogs and luncheon meats.
Breads and starches: wheat, spelt, kamut, corn, rye and barley.
Vegetables: corn, legumes (beans, peas and soy products)
Fruit: Oranges citrus, apples and their juices. You can use pineapple, tomato.
Sweets: All sweeteners and food products containing added sugar. You will also need to avoid most packaged and processed foods as they usually contain sugar, food colouring and other additives. Chocolate containing foods.
Beverages: apple juice, orange and citrus juice. Coffee, tea and alcohol. Soft drinks.

Symptoms of Allergy

Almost any chronic symptom can be caused by an allergic reaction, although allergy does not necessarily cause all of these symptoms. It is sometimes difficult to distinguish between allergic and nonallergic symptoms. Many people with persistent symptoms, who have been from doctor to doctor without relief, or who are told that their problems are in their heads, have problems caused by food allergy. Most people who have hypoglycemic symptoms, or suspect they have the Candida yeast syndrome, are allergic to certain foods. Many illnesses not directly caused by allergies, such as chronic bronchitis, emphysema, scleroderma and lupus, can be worsened by allergic reactions.

Abdominal Symptoms

Food allergy in the bowel can cause a variety of symptoms. Reactions in the gastro-intestinal tract follow the usual allergy pattern; swelling, excess secretion, increased muscular spasm and pain. These symptoms may start soon after eating or hours or even days later. Sometimes the tongue or lips will swell shortly after eating the allergenic food. Swelling can cause irregular bowel function and pain. Excess secretion and increased muscular spasm can cause diarrhea. Diarrhea, abdominal pain, nausea and vomiting are common food allergy symptoms. Very often these problems will start in the first months of a baby's life. If these continue for an extended period the bowel may not absorb enough nutrients to allow for a child's growth. He may lose weight or not grow as expected. About one-third of infants with chronic diarrhea caused by cow's milk will still be sensitive to cow's milk four to ten years later and will often develop inhalant allergies. When an infant's or toddler's chronic diarrhea contains blood and mucous, frequently food allergy especially to milk and eggs is responsible. Infantile colitis can appear in breast or formula fed babies. Treatment requires changing the foods that mother eats or using a hypoallergenic formula such as Nutramigen or Good Start. In adults all of the same symptoms may appear because of food reactions. In addition, some people with irritable bowel disease, ulcerative colitis and Crohn's disease have symptoms caused by reactions to specific foods. Recurrent peptic ulcers have been traced to allergic reactions. Excessive gas and bloating or digestive difficulties are frequently signs of an allergic reaction. An allergic reaction may masquerade as a bowel infection that does not clear up. Abdominal pain with diarrhea and hives can be the result of dye in medications and food.

If the allergic reaction takes place soon after an allergenic food is eaten, there is usually little problem in identifying the allergen. If the reaction occurs several hours later, it may be difficult to decide if the problem is one of allergy at all. Because there may be several food allergies present, eliminating one food such as milk or soy may not clear up the problem. It may be necessary to eliminate several foods at once.

Allergic bowel disease should be suspected in any child or adult with any bowel symptoms that do not clear up as expected after a short course of treatment especially when X-rays and tests do not show any disease. Allergy in the bowel needs to be distinguished from symptoms caused by lactose intolerance and celiac disease (see below).

Colic

Colic is a syndrome in which an otherwise healthy baby has many episodes of unexplained crying, irritability or fussing during the first three months of life. The episodes last ½ to 2 hours or more. They usually go on for several hours per day and for several days per week. The cause of colic is not known and there has been no standard treatment. It can be very upsetting to parents who want to calm a baby who is very uncomfortable.

Some medical researchers feel that it is the result of a baby responding to the early anxieties and uncertainties of new parents. They feel that if the parents are relaxed then the baby will be less colicky. Yet colic seems to have appeared only in the past 100 years since the general introduction of cow's milk for baby feeding. Higher levels of cow milk protein are found in the breast milk of mothers drinking cow's milk with colicky infants and may be a cause of colic. Stopping cow's milk will help many formula fed babies lose their colicky symptoms. Breast fed babies often improve if mother stops the use of dairy products. As an alternative to cow's milk formula, soy milk or a predigested cow's milk formula such as Good Start or Nutramigen could be used. Remember, that soy milk allergy is also common. It may not be the best cow's milk replacement.

To help settle a colicky baby it is often helpful to hold the baby face downwards with your arms supporting her. Keep the pressure of your arms off her abdomen and rock her just as you would if she were face upwards. This will soothe many babies within several minutes.

Lactose Intolerance

Lactose is a complex sugar made of two simple sugars, glucose and galactose. Lactose is present in the milk of all mammals except some seals and walruses. To be absorbed, lactose must first be digested into its two component sugars. Lactose intolerance is the result of the loss from the bowel wall of the enzyme lactase that digests lactose. Undigested lactose inside the bowel causes the passage of water into the small intestine and the colon. This results in increased activity by the bowel as it tries to expel the fluid. Bacteria in the lower bowel digest the lactose releasing hydrogen gas and organic acids. This results in the gas, diarrhea, bloating, acid stools and abdominal pain 30 to 60 minutes after eating dairy products. Some dairy products such as cheese or yogurt may contain less lactose than milk and may not cause problems.

Lactose intolerance is inherited and is very common particularly in Asians, indigenous Americans, blacks and Europeans whose ancestors come from the Mediterranean basin. An infant will inherit the predisposition to lactose intolerance but usually will be tolerant of milk in the early years. As he grows he will slowly lose the ability to digest dairy products.

Lactose intolerance can be diagnosed by measuring the hydrogen in the breath or by measuring blood glucose levels after eating dairy products. But, a simpler method could be to check for lactose intolerance by drinking two glasses of milk. If you have increased gas, bloating or diarrhea try the same milk but take Lactaid (a product that contains lactase the enzyme missing in the bowel) before drinking it. Compare the effects. If Lactaid prevents the symptoms then lactose intolerance is probably the cause of the symptoms and Lactaid can be used before consuming dairy products. If it does not help then the symptoms could be the result of an allergic reaction.

Celiac Disease

Gluten is a protein found in wheat, rye, barley, spelt and oats. Gluten itself is made up of glutenin and gliadin. There are four types of gliadin present in gluten. Some people, perhaps because of an inherited inability to digest gliadin completely, will develop symptoms when they eat these grains caused by a direct toxic effect of the undigested gliadin on the bowel wall. The symptoms that develop may be diarrhea, abdominal bloating, gas, nausea, vomiting, tongue and mouth sores. Because of the inability to absorb food nutrients properly there may be weight loss or a child may not grow properly. Rashes and vitamin deficiencies may appear. Commonly people with celiac disease have blue eyes and fair hair. It is important to diagnose celiac disease accurately because it is a lifelong problem that requires permanent avoidance of the above grains. Although allergy does not cause celiac disease, allergies to wheat and other foods may also be present.

Asthma and Lung Disease

If allergic reactions affect the lungs, the bronchial tubes can become inflamed, constrict and produce excessive mucous. This can cause asthma symptoms: wheezing, coughing and shortness of breath. and leave the lungs are generally more sensitive. They will react to nonspecific irritants such as cold air, street dust or chemicals. Exercise can provoke cough, wheeze or shortness of breath in persons with asthma. Children living in homes with smokers or gas stoves are more likely to have more breathing problems. Children living in homes with dampness or mould problems tend to have more respiratory illness, cough, wheezing and asthma.

Sometimes allergen exposure may not be obvious. For example, there can be enough cat and dog allergen sticking to clothing worn to school by nonallergic children that children allergic to cat and dog start to wheeze. The solution may be as simple as having the chairs at school cleaned regularly to prevent allergen build up. Similarly almost all homes of asthmatics have been found to contain cat allergen even if a cat has never been in the home.

Recurrent croup is a common disease in children caused by a viral infection. It can cause difficult, noisy breathing. Children with recurrent croup have a high frequency of allergy and over reactive airways.

Asthma

The end of the twentieth century has witnessed a surge in the prevalence of asthma and in the number of deaths due to asthma. It is the most common childhood chronic disease. Research studies show that asthmatics, whether severely or mildly affected, who most use and overuse some of these medications are at the greatest risk of dying from breathing problems. The prevalence of asthma in children under 18, in the U.S.A. increased from 1981 to 1988 from 3.1% to 4.3%.

This arises from the complicated nature of asthma. The predisposition for developing asthma is inherited. But there are two major elements to the appearance of asthma. First, there is inflammation in the cells lining the bronchioles, the small airways of the lung. Inflammation causes the cells to swell and secrete mucous into the airway. The membrane lining the airway is damaged. The tiny muscle cells around the airway enlarge and white blood cells enter the tissue. The amount of air that can enter the lungs is reduced.

Second, when the lungs are irritated by allergens such as dust, animal dander or pollen, by viral infections or by smoke the muscles around the bronchioles contract narrowing the already cramped passages. Even less air can enter. The results are shortness of breath, wheezing sounds as the air rushes through constricted passages and perhaps coughing. Asthma should be suspected in a child or adult with repeated episodes of shortness of breath or if a cough persists without any other signs of infection.

If you have an episode of asthma, start treating it early on. Most asthmatic children will have mild warning symptoms six hours or more before the onset of an asthmatic episode. These symptoms are usually the same each time. This would be the time to start treatment to prevent a worse episode from developing.

If you are using bronchodilator drugs more than a couple times a week and especially if you use them several times a day check with your doctor to see if you can start to switch over, partly or completely, to anti-inflammatory medications. Sodium cromoglycate, nedocromil and corticosteroids work more slowly to relieve asthma than bronchodilators. They do not work immediately but they do alleviate inflammation. If used regularly they can be very helpful to prevent asthma attacks after about one week of use. Although sodium cromoglycate is safe, corticosteroids have the potential to cause side effects if taken over a long period in large amounts particularly in children. Growth may be slowed and adrenal hormone excretion may be altered. Try to start with anti-inflammatory sprays that are not based on corticosteroids. You may want to stop all medications but this may not be possible especially if you have had asthma for many years.

Next, find out what your allergies are and bring them under control. Allergies can be the major or one of many provokers of asthma. Once tested, stay away from food allergens. Control dust mites, mould, pollens and animal hair to the best of your ability. Air pollutants, either outdoor or indoor can be strong irritants in the lungs. Be especially careful to avoid cigarette smoke. Many people find that perfumes smells or incense can trigger asthma.

Asthma that occurs usually at night may be caused by dust mites in the pillows, mattress or bedding. A hot water wash (above $55°C/130°F$) or a hot dryer cycle can kill the mites. You will want to avoid colds and flus as much as you can so keep yourself fit and unstressed. Wash your hands a lot if you are around people who are sick. Many viruses are transmitted through physical contact and not through the air. If you are starting to get a cold try sucking on a 25 mg. zinc gluconate lozenge every two hours, up to six a day. Often it will stop or at least diminish a cold.

Some people, children or adults, may have a persistent dry cough with no wheeze or shortness of breath as the only sign of asthma. The cough is the result of irritation to nerve fibres in the lungs caused by inflammation. The cough may be mild or interfere with normal activities. Tests such as X-rays or breathing tests may be normal. When tests are normal a trial of oral anti-inflammatory medications for several days may stop the cough and guide further treatment.

Smoking is very dangerous for people with asthma. Smokers die more frequently from their asthma than nonsmokers. Food additives such as sulphites, MSG, tartrazine and benzoates can provoke asthma in sensitive people. Sulphites are preservative chemicals used in beverages, fruits, vegetables and medications. They can provoke asthma in susceptible people and should be avoided. Unfortunately even if sulphites are in foods they may not appear on the label. They may be sprayed on foods at a salad bar or in stores. They are present in just about all wines and many alcoholic beverages. They may be added to canned fruits and vegetables and to dried fruits. The label may say sulphur dioxide or metabisulphite. The list below indicates some common hidden sources of sulphites.

Foods Commonly Treated with Sulphites

Avocado dip, guacamole

Beverages: beer, cider, colas, ginger ale, wine, orange drinks

Cake mixes, bread and roll mixes, cookies and pie dough

Canned, bottled or frozen fruit juices

Cheese spreads, Brie cheese

Dried cod, shellfish (fresh, frozen, canned or dried)

Fruit (pre-sliced, dried, fillings, frozen or preserved)

Gelatin

Instant tea and coffee

Mushrooms (fresh or canned)

Pizza and pasta

Potatoes (pre-sliced, dried, canned or frozen)

Salad dressing, relishes

Salads, especially salad bars

Sauces and gravies (canned or dried)

Sauerkraut, cole slaw, pickles

Snack foods

Soups (canned or dried)

Sugar, corn syrup, pancake, syrup

Vegetables (pre-sliced, dried, canned or frozen)

Vinegar: wine or cider

Asthma treatment is usually most effective if you take several approaches at once. Food allergens will need to be eliminated. Inhalant allergens should be controlled by thoroughly cleaning up the environment or by using allergen immunotherapy. Nonspecific irritants such as cigarette smoke, air pollution, outdoor dust and gastro-esophageal reflux will need to be controlled. When children are no longer exposed to their parents smoking their asthma symptoms diminish. Acid from the stomach can drip up into the esophagus and into the lungs during sleep. This is a factor in about 10% of children and adults with difficult to control asthma. It can be helped by raising the head of the bed 4 or 5 inches or by using medication. If allergens are avoided completely, it is possible for asthma to improve dramatically.

Studies have shown that extra Vitamin C and Vitamin B_6 reduce the frequency and severity of airway constriction and asthma episodes but may not help those on steroid medications. A high salt intake is associated with increased wheezing. High dietary niacin and a high ratio of zinc to copper in the diet is associated with lower rates of wheezing. Reducing salt intake may help the asthmatic condition. Blood levels of selenium and the enzyme it functions with, glutathione peroxidase, are both low in asthmatics. Magnesium may help to relax the bronchiolar muscles. See page 58 for a list of foods which contain these nutrients.

Eczema and Skin Disease

Eczema/Atopic Dermatitis

Classic allergic eczema, also called atopic dermatitis, begins in 60% of affected people in the first year of life but after two months of age. A child may develop dryness of the skin that progresses to severe itchiness. Constant scratching of the dry areas, that otherwise look normal, leads to the appearance of the characteristic red, scaly rash. It is the scratching that brings out the visible rash. If the person did not scratch the rash would not be as intense. Often scratching will go on while the child or adult is asleep. The itch can be so strong that the scratching can cause bleeding. Usually the rash first appears on a child's face, scalp, chest, arms or legs. Later in life, often after ten years of age, the rash may appear anywhere. It may be on the face, arms, back or the back of the hands and feet. Often small white bumps that contain a colourless fluid precede the rash.

The exact biochemical cause of atopic dermatitis is not known although allergy to foods or dust mites will often provoke it. In children with extremely bad eczema not responding to usual treatments about 75% improve with pet and dust mite avoidance combined with a very strict allergen avoidance diet. Homes of people with atopic dermatitis have higher numbers of dust mites. In fact a variety of airborne allergens have been found to aggravate eczema. These include tree, grass and weed pollens, dust mite, mould and animal danders. One study found that the skin reacted to contact with these airborne allergens. It may be that airborne allergens penetrate the skin causing the development of itchiness. Even food allergens that are transferred from foods mother eats to her breast milk can aggravate eczema. Cow's milk allergens can be identified in mother's milk. Removal of milk from mother's diet can lead to improvement in baby's eczema.

Scratching will cause the release of chemicals in the skin, such as histamine, which will increase the itch and cause skin inflammation. A vicious cycle will develop with more scratching and worsening of the skin. The inflamed skin may become infected with bacteria or yeasts that may aggravate the inflammation further.

Atopic dermatitis appears more frequently in highly industrialized countries and in families with a history of allergy and eczema. From 1946 to 1970 there was an increase in reported eczema of over 100% in Britain. The same doubling in the incidence of eczema has also been found in Denmark. This suggests that there may be some environmental factor such as a pollutant in food, water or air increasing the incidence of eczema.

Some researchers theorize that an abnormality in skin fatty acid metabolism may be part of the cause. Atopic dermatitis in children and adults can sometimes be successfully treated with evening primrose oil. This is a good source of a special fatty acid, gamma linoleic acid that may correct the abnormality. You could use 500 mg. per year of age per day or eight daily for adults.

Any itchy rash will be less bothersome if the skin is kept cool and moist. A good moisturizer that does not irritate the skin and is not greasy should be used regularly. You probably will need to try several different brands before you find one that is acceptable. Apply it generously immediately after a bath or shower.

Hives

Hives or urticaria are itchy, raised, red patches on the skin. The itch can be intense but when the hive settles down it will leave no scar. Hives can be the result of an allergic reaction to almost anything. They can be caused by food, medications, chemicals, food additives, infections, other illnesses, pollens, animal danders, mould or dust mites. They also can be caused by mechanical irritation on the skin such as heat, cold, vibration, pressure or water contact. Sometimes they are the result of a nervous system reaction to stressful events or chronic stress.

When hives appear for the first time it is often easy to find the cause. But when they have been present for several months tracking down the cause can become very difficult. It may then be necessary to search for allergy to foods, food additives, inhalants or chemicals. Chronic infection with viruses, parasites, fungi or bacteria may be responsible. Underlying disease may be a factor. Hives can be caused by the action of bacteria in the bowel on a high carbohydrate diet. Fortunately a variety of medications are available to control the hives even if the cause cannot be readily discovered.

Hayfever, Rhinitis and Nasal Symptoms

Allergic reactions to food or inhalants can affect the nose, sinuses, ears or throat. In response to allergic provocation the mucous membranes lining the nose can swell, blocking the nose or the allergy may cause a watery discharge. There can be sniffles, a stuffy or itchy nose, repeated nose bleeds, mouth breathing or snoring. If the lining of the sinuses swells and the channels for drainage of the sinuses are obstructed, pain and a chronic sinus infection may follow. Polyps, outgrowths of tissue in the nose, can result from allergic reactions. Some children get a line across their nose from rubbing it so frequently and vigorously. Nasal allergy can reduce the sense of smell. About 25 to 50% of people with hayfever or year round nasal congestion have a reduced sense of smell. People with nasal polyps or chronic sinus infection are even more likely to have impaired sense of smell.

If the nose is very congested breathing can become difficult during sleep. This can lead to snoring or complete but temporary obstruction of breathing. This is termed sleep apnea. Sleep apnea can cause daytime fatigue and problems with behaviour, mood, blood pressure and sleep.

Hayfever may seem to be merely a mild annoyance but school children with hayfever are often more apathetic, absent minded or disinterested in their school activities. These children do not learn as well as their nonallergic classmates.

Eyes, Ears and Mouth

Allergy can cause the mucous membranes of the throat to become swollen and painful. A mucous discharge in the throat can have drained from the nose and cause frequent throat clearing or shallow coughing. Frequent recurrent sore throats also can be the result of allergic reactions. Whenever the mucous membranes of the nose or throat are swollen or inflamed by an allergic reaction they become more susceptible to invasion by viruses and bacteria. Therefore, frequent colds, tonsillitis and upper respiratory infections also can be indirectly caused by allergy. When the nasal passages are obstructed by the swelling of mucous membranes children or adults may be forced to breathe through their mouths. A long term result of mouth breathing is permanent change in the shape of the face. The palate may become high and arched and the chin and upper face may become narrow. An overbite may develop. By the age of five or ten it may be too late to change these facial changes by allergy management.

The conjunctiva is the external lining of the eye. With allergy it can get inflamed and produce a discharge or become red or swollen. Often the area below the eyes will appear dark and puffy as blood pools there. This is due to delayed emptying of the veins in the congested allergic membranes of the nose. Chronic congestion below the eyes can lead to allergic eye creases just under the lower lids.

Because of allergic reactions the eustachian tube between the throat and the inner ear can become swollen and blocked off. This creates a pressure difference between the outer ear and the inner ear and blocks drainage of fluid form the middle ear. Fluid builds up in the ear and pain, pressure or loss of hearing acuity occurs. Yawning briefly opens the eustachian tube so you hear crackling or popping sounds. If there are bacteria in the ear when the eustachian tube is congested, a middle ear infection can result. Children with frequent ear infections often will have allergy as the underlying cause.

Allergy to food sometimes causes vertigo (dizziness), hearing loss and tinnitus (noise in the ears). This triad of symptoms is called Meniere's disease. Animal experiments have shown that it can be the result of allergic reactions that occur in the inner ear.

There are no specific allergens that cause specific reactions in any one area. Allergens such as food, dust mould or anything else can affect the eyes, ears, nose, chest or any other organ. But milk is often the responsible allergen when young children have frequent ear infections. Before myringotomy tubes are used to treat recurrent ear infections, even if no other allergy investigation is done, it is very often helpful to remove all dairy products from a child's diet.

Itching in the mouth and throat or around the mouth can be caused by reactions to food, usually fruits and vegetables. Often these are foods that cross-react with pollens. For example, birch pollen allergy can be associated with symptoms from apple, hazelnut, peach, carrot, celery, plums, almond, potato, walnut, peanut, cherry, pear, apricot, coconut, turnip, tomato or kiwi. Ragweed allergy with cantaloupe, honeydew melon, watermelon and banana. Mugwort allergy with celery, carrot, caraway, dill, parsley, fennel, green pepper and aniseed. This is called the oral allergy syndrome. In this syndrome immunotherapy of the pollen has been found to help control the food symptoms.

Headaches

Migraine headaches are common in both children and adults. They most commonly first arise between the ages of six to ten. Migraines are a severe type of throbbing headache that are often located in the front or side of the head. They are sometimes accompanied by an aura of visual or sensory alterations. Often there is nausea and vomiting and a dislike of bright light. Sometimes there is also abdominal pain and even fever. Frequently migraines run in families. The headache arises from irritability and abnormal expansion and contraction of blood vessels. This can be triggered by many things but reactions to food are a common inciting factor. These reactions may be allergic or nonallergic in nature. Some children and adults will react to naturally occurring chemicals in foods such as tyramine or phenylethylamine or food additives such as MSG or nitrates. These chemicals cause headaches by way of their biochemical activity on blood vessels.

Most people are aware that heavy coffee drinkers will have a headache for a few days if they suddenly stop drinking coffee. The headache will stop quickly if coffee is resumed. But this headache can also occur in people drinking only two cups a day. The headache can be accompanied by anxiety and fatigue. If you do get a headache on stopping even low levels of coffee intake, it is a good idea not to drink it every day or eliminate it entirely; it may be the cause of chronic symptoms.

Children with both migraine headaches and uncontrolled epilepsy have been found to lose their seizures when their food and food additive allergens are avoided.

Behaviour, Mood and Nervous System

One of the most distressing and common behavioral problems in children and also adults is the attention deficit hyperactivity disorder (ADHD). It is characterized by difficulties with paying attention, with organizing tasks, with sustained attention, distractibility, fidgeting and lack of impulse control. Males are affected five to ten times more often than females. It is important to be sure that these children do not have visual or hearing problems or learning disabilities and that there are no neuropsychological problems. No one knows what causes ADHD, there may be several different causes, but there are many ways to try to bring the abnormal behaviour under control. Traditionally doctors have prescribed medication and social changes but there are alternatives that can be very effective.

A good first step in treatment is to take all sugars out of the diet. Fruits and a little unsweetened juice can be used but no sugar, honey, maple syrup or other sweeteners. All food colours, additives and artificial flavours should be avoided. Nutritional treatment for ADHD goes back to the diet introduced by Dr. Ben Feingold in 1973. This diet removed salicylate containing foods and artificial food colours and flavours. His theory was that some children had genetic variations that made them susceptible to these chemicals. Sensitive children would need to avoid them for life. It was effective for 30 to 50% of children treated.

The role of food allergy in ADHD was suggested in the 1930's and 40's but was not tested and shown to be significant until the 1970's. Not only food allergy but allergy to airborne allergens such as mould may be part of the problem. It is important that children with ADHD caused by allergy be treated as early as possible. The earlier in a child's life that the change is made the more likely it is to succeed. As the children get older they can learn self-destructive behaviour patterns that will be very difficult to change.

Children with ADHD are more likely to get ear infections and earaches than other children. This may reflect the allergic nature of both problems. Frequently other behaviour problems and school problems in children are related to food reactions.

Adults frequently complain of fatigue and depression unrelated to the degree of exertion or emotional stress. The fatigue may be worse after meals or temporarily relieved by food only to recur several hours later. There are many possible causes of this chronic fatigue but when no illness is present, food allergy is often responsible. Many people with hayfever find that during their allergy season that they experience increased fatigue as well as decreased concentration, irritability and temper tantrums.

When allergy affects the nervous system, there may be symptoms such as tiredness, malaise, mood changes or behavioral changes. Symptoms that are thought to be related to hypoglycaemia such as fatigue, shakiness, giddiness or cravings for food are often allergy induced.

In children with chronic insomnia, if no other cause for the insomnia is found, removing milk from the diet can result in improvement in sleeping within weeks. Adults who severely over sleep and snore have been found to have food allergy as the cause of their problems.

There are case reports of depression being alleviated when allergens were removed from the patient's life. Fatigue and psychological symptoms such as depression, anger and confusion can result from food allergen challenge. For some people allergy symptoms can be so severe that psychological distress can be a secondary result of the symptoms caused by allergy. The reverse also can occur, people with emotional difficulties can appear to have problems caused by allergy. On closer examination some of these people are found to have psychological problems that are disguised as allergy symptoms.

Urinary and Genital Symptoms

Bed wetting can be the result of food allergy. The allergic reaction may leave the bladder irritable and more likely to contract uncontrollably after the child eats an allergic food. When the reaction is delayed for a few hours after eating dinner, later in the night the bed will be wet. Milk is often responsible. In adults a nonspecific irritation of the bladder called interstitial cystitis can be caused by allergy. Weight gain caused by fluid retention without a known cause is frequently caused by allergy and may disappear very quickly when the allergens are removed.

Recent studies have shown that some women with recurrent vaginal infections have antibodies to food and inhalant allergens in their vaginal secretions. These women have fewer infections when their allergies are controlled or when using allergy medication.

Arthritis, Joint and Muscle Pains

Allergy to food can cause swelling, pain or stiffness in the joints or muscles. When the pains are fleeting, moving from joint to joint, it is called palindromic arthritis. Sometimes allergic reactions to food can mimic severe arthritis. About 5% of patients with rheumatic disease have symptoms provoked by allergy to foods. Milk, shrimp and nitrates are the major provokers. Although swelling may improve quickly it can take two or three years of allergen avoidance for arthritis pain to stop.

Candida/Yeast Syndrome

In 1978, Dr. Orion Truss published a report on 6 patients. The patients had symptoms in many parts of their bodies. These symptoms were apparently unrelated to yeast infections and had not responded to other treatment. But they had improved when treated with antifungal medication. The yeast syndrome, as Dr. Truss described it, is caused by an overgrowth of Candida yeasts in the intestinal tract. He states that yeasts first establish a firm beachhead in the bowel. Then yeast allergens pass through the bowel wall resulting in the development of an allergy to the yeast and allergic reactions at distant sites. The symptoms that can be caused by the yeast syndrome can affect any part of the body. They are frequently accompanied by psychological symptoms such as depression or anxiety.

There is evidence supporting various aspects of the yeast syndrome theory. Most physicians are aware of and have treated Candida overgrowth on mucous membranes that is the result of treatment with antibiotics, oral contraceptives, or steroid medications. By encouraging yeast growth they may promote the development of hypersensitivity to Candida. Antibodies to Candida proteins and carbohydrates can be found in patients with rhinitis and asthma. Allergic reactions to Candida antigen were shown in 20% of asthmatics in one study. Trichophyton is another important fungal antigen since it too is commonly found on human tissues. In some patients Candida and Trichophyton have been suggested as the cause of a variety of diseases such as asthma, hives, psoriasis, colitis etc. Allergy to Candida is one cause of chronic vaginal infection as is persistence of Candida in the intestine. Antifungal medications and immunotherapy can help some patients with these problems. These illnesses are not caused by simple Candida infections but hypersensitivity, allergy or difficulty in killing off Candida. Although yeasts may in some people cause some of these problems (perhaps even through immunologic mechanisms) this does not amount to proof of the existence of the syndrome.

Among the difficulties with the Candida syndrome theory is the lack of an accurate diagnostic test. Several blood tests have been developed but none are sufficiently accurate. This is because almost everyone has had contact with Candida yeasts during their life time and retain antibodies against Candida in their blood. Questionnaires are used in many books about the yeast syndrome but they are much too general to be of use in making a diagnosis.

A further problem relates to the microbiology of bowel yeasts. The above books claim that not eating high carbohydrate foods will influence the course of the syndrome. Many patients are unwell almost immediately after eating some of these foods. Even if the general theory is accurate, it is unlikely that yeast cells present in the bowel would grow and release antigens within an hour or less of eating. Medical reports on the growth response of Candida to carbohydrate foods are divided. One report showed increased numbers of Candida cells in the bowel, another no change and a third diminished growth. Malnutrition however is a consistent stimulant to Candida growth. Sugar is the only consistent dietary factor which has been shown to increase the frequency of vaginal yeast infection.

Many people find that following the diet recommended in the yeast syndrome books helps their symptoms. Because the diet removes most of the common allergens and since diet, except for sugar intake, is not likely to make any difference to yeast growth, it is probable that most people who feel better following these diets have a food allergy problem. In a study of patients who thought that they had the yeast syndrome, patients were tested and placed on allergen avoidance diets. Three quarters of the patients had a good or partial response to elimination of dietary allergens. This study suggests that most of those who believe that they have the yeast syndrome have problems caused by food hypersensitivity

Preventing Allergy

Primary Prevention

There are three very important steps to preventing the development of allergy. The first is breast feeding. A Finnish study published in the Lancet in 1995 found that breast feeding for a minimum of six months reduced the prevalence of allergy symptoms such as eczema, food allergy and respiratory allergy at 17 years by about one-third. Even breast feeding for shorter periods helped reduce the frequency of allergy at that age. Other recent studies have found that breast feeding plus avoidance of common allergens can also have a major impact. A mother who avoids common allergenic foods such as milk, egg, fish and nuts while breast feeding an infant who avoids these plus soy, wheat and orange when he starts to eat, combined with eliminating dust mite in the infant's bedroom can reduce the amount of allergic illness by two-thirds at one year of age. Compared to formula fed infants, by eighteen months children who have been breast fed or used a hypoallergenic formula and who have not been exposed to tobacco smoke, pets, carpeted floors and damp rooms have one-third as much wheezing, half the eczema, a quarter the vomiting or diarrhea, half the ear infections, one-third the colic and one-third the food allergy. However using just one formula feeding per day can eliminate the allergy prevention benefit of breast feeding.

The means by which breast feeding prevents the development of allergy are not well understood. It may be that breast milk enhances the maturation of an infant's bowel wall and immune system. This would prevent the entrance of foreign food allergens into the body. Antibodies that are present in mother's milk may reduce the risk of allergy by blocking the development of immunoglobulin E antibodies (the type of antibody often associated with allergy) to foods. Cow specific antibodies are present in cow's milk formula but they are not effective in preventing allergy and may increase the risk of allergy developing. Soy milk formula does not contain any antibodies.

If you have decided to breast feed to help prevent allergy in your baby, insist that your baby not be given formula while mother is in the hospital. Formula is often given, without your knowledge, in the hospital nursery so as not to disturb mother's rest. If you can, have your baby room-in at the hospital. Remember that formula milk is not the equal of breast milk.

For mothers unable to breast feed there are now available commercially several alternatives to regular cow's milk and soy formula. They are referred to as hypoallergenic formula since they reduce the likelihood of developing reactions to milk. There are two older products, Nutramigen introduced in 1942 and Pregestimil which are casein derived and a newer formula Good Start derived from whey. All three of these are hydrolysed ie. pre-digested. This process breaks down the milk proteins into smaller sub-units which are less likely to cause an allergic reaction or to set off the development of a milk allergy. Good Start is less hydrolysed than the others. As a result it is less well tolerated by babies who are already allergic to cow's milk. For new born babies up to three months of age Pregestimil is more appropriate than Nutramigen because of its different amino acid balance. After three months either can be used. Good Start can be used at any age. Simply heating cow's milk will not destroy its allergenicity.

All of these pre-digested formula are less likely than regular milk formula to cause reactions in milk allergic babies and to cause the development of milk allergy. You can cut by half or more the chances of your formula fed baby developing cow's milk allergy by using a predigested milk. The benefit of six months of a hypoallergenic formula can still be found at three years of age and if it is continued and regular milk avoided the benefit may be maintained. However none of them is 100% guaranteed to not cause reactions in babies who are already very sensitive to cow's milk. Caution is required if your baby is already having severe reactions to cow's milk formula and you wish to try one of these products. Nutramigen is less likely than Good Start to cause reactions in infants whoare already allergic to milk.

What are the other advantages of breast feeding? Breast milk contains a variety of proteins including antibodies derived from mother's immune system that will help protect baby from many types of infections. There are over twenty distinct substances in breast milk that help fight off infections. This may be another factor in the prevention of allergy. Breast milk has certain carbohydrates that promote the growth of normal bacteria in the bowel. It also creates a more acidic bowel environment that promotes the growth of these essential bacteria. Mucin, the slippery part of mucus, is found in breast milk and helps protect babies from bouts of viral diarrhea. It is not found in formula milk. Breast fed children get fewer urinary tract infections. If breast fed only for four months they also get 40% fewer middle ear infections.

Giving the baby supplemental bottle feeds and using a pacifier in the first weeks, may gradually decrease the amount of milk that is produced. Avoid pacifiers and allow your baby to breast feed on demand from the very beginning. Newborns should be given only breast milk with no other food or drink unless they are sick. Try to stay with your baby 24 hours a day while in the hospital. Ask for help in breast feeding within 30 minutes of giving birth. Don't stop feeding if your baby gets diarrhea. Breast feeding is the best treatment for a gut infection.

The second important step is the avoidance of airborne allergens. Infants exposed to cats and dogs during the first year of life tend to develop allergy later in life, more often than unexposed infants. Similarly, children born during the pollination season of plants have a higher risk of developing allergy to those plant pollens. The allergy may appear 20 to 30 years later. This may also be true of dust mite and mould allergens. Maintaining a low allergen environment, particularly in the first years of life may be very beneficial.

The third important step is reducing exposure to indoor and outdoor airborne pollutants. Exposing a person to pollutants such as cigarette smoke or diesel exhaust can increase the rate of allergic sensitization in both children and adults. A study of animals exposed to cigarette smoke and inhalant allergens (such as dust or pollen) at the same time showed that they have an increased likelihood that allergy to the inhalant will appear. If either one or both parents smoke, your child will have a greater likelihood of allergy developing. In addition, the amount of smoking in a child's home is in direct proportion to the degree of breathlessness that an asthmatic child will experience.

Secondary Prevention

It is plainly to late for anyone reading this to be practising primary allergy prevention. But there are still several things you can do to prevent the appearance of more allergies. It may seem too obvious to mention but avoiding allergies that you know of will prevent them from causing stronger reactions in the future. Some people feel that if their allergic reactions are minor then they can just ignore them. If ignored, over time an allergen can cause increasing trouble. It is also useful to avoid foods that cross-react with your known allergens. The list on page 8 will help to guide you. The other benefit of avoiding known food allergens is that if you avoid a non-fixed food allergen for long enough, it may stop reacting. You can determine if you have lost a reaction to a food by challenging that food every three to six months. Instructions on how to challenge a food are on page 12. If you do not react to the food during the test days, then you could eat that food but no more frequently than once in three or four days on rotation. This will help to prevent the re-development of an allergy to that food.

There are several life-style factors that are known to enhance the development of allergy. These are poor nutritional balance, everyday consumption of alcohol, excess or insufficient sleep, smoking, irregular daily life patterns, working over 9 hours daily and a strong feeling of mental stress.

Although you and your children may not smoke you will be affected by the side-stream smoke given off by smokers. Smoke contains hundreds of potent and dangerous chemicals. People with allergies, when not allergic to tobacco smoke, are more sensitive to the irritant effects of the smoke on their lungs and nasal tissues. Children exposed to smoke tend to have more frequent and severe respiratory problems. Smoke interferes with the immune response towards infections. Tobacco smoke can increase the severity and the frequency of allergic reactions in smokers and children of smokers.

Alcohol causes allergy problems for many people. In addition to allergens from grains, grape or yeast in alcoholic beverages the alcohol itself affects the lining of the bowel, making it more porous. This speeds up the absorption of food allergens. The result can be more rapid and more severe reactions to food allergens in the beverage as well as to those eaten with the alcoholic beverage.

The immune system does not operate in isolation from the rest of the body. Events that affect your body and mind can affect the function of the immune system. Recent research has shown just how closely the mind, body and immune system are connected. Researchers have found that there are receptors on the white blood cells of the immune system for chemicals that are produced in the brain. The reverse of this has also been shown; there are receptors on the surface of brain cells for chemicals produced by cells of the immune system. This means that when we are under stress or experiencing psychological distress the chemicals that the brain produces to cope with this can affect how the immune system operates. It is well known to doctors that people will have stronger allergic reactions at these times. When allergic people are reacting they may have changes in their thinking process and emotional state.

This means that there can be increased allergic reactions when the body is under increased physical or emotional stress. Many people do not understand this intimate connection. As a result many people and doctors may say that allergies are all in the mind. This is an unfortunate misunderstanding of the synchronized inter-action of the mind and body.

Conditioning is a process in which an initially neutral stimulus is paired with another stimulus (the unconditioned stimulus) that always produces an unconditioned response. After several pairings of the two stimuli an association between the two is formed. After the association is formed the previously neutral stimulus will produce the unconditioned response. Immune responses can be conditioned and this has been shown to affect antibody production, several types of white blood cell growth and inflammation. A conditioned stimulus can also effect breathing, itch, skin redness and dislike of tastes. Some reactions that appear to be allergies may be conditioned responses. Conditioned responses may fade away if the initially neutral stimulus is repeated frequently without pairing with an unconditioned stimulus.

Stress can produce reactions that appear to be allergic although they are not caused by immune system reactions. Some people, when under stress, unconsciously will start to breath very rapidly and shallowly. This is called hyperventilation. Hyperventilation results in a lowered amount of carbon dioxide in the blood and lowered body acidity. The change in acid level causes nerves and muscles to become more irritable. The resulting symptoms can be a feeling of tightness in the chest or inability to take a proper breath. There can be giddiness, numbness or tingling in the arms or legs and sometimes muscle cramps. Sometimes there are strong feelings of anxiety, sweating or shaking. If the stressful situation is not resolved, hyperventilation can become the usual reaction to situations of even mild stress. Hyperventilation can be triggered by the stress of going out to meet people or going shopping. Because many people are unaware that they are hyperventilating they may feel that they are having allergic reactions to a wide variety of situations and substances. Their symptoms usually will disappear when they learn how to deal with stress and when they learn more beneficial breathing patterns.

Frequently people are not aware that they are under stress. Stressful situations may have been going on for such a long time that they begin to feel routine. But problems that relate to the situations may come to the surface in the twenties, thirties or even later in life. Children raised in homes where alcoholism, drug abuse, physical, sexual, verbal or emotional abuse were occurring often learn counter-productive coping patterns. They may find themselves, later in life, in relationships that mimic the difficult relationships of their childhood. They may develop physical disease or symptoms that do not respond to treatment. They may seem to become allergic to many environmental factors. Sadly, because there are treatments available, some people do not recognize the source of their symptoms or even clearly remember the painful events of the past since they have been coping for so long with the unresolved emotional difficulty.

Wheat Foods

Baked Items

Bagels, biscuits, bread, crackers, johnny cake, muffins, pancakes, pretzels, rolls, rusks, sweet rolls, waffles, zwieback. Prepared mixes for any of these. All bakery goods. Any of these made with other flours may also contain wheat flour. Check labels carefully.

Beverages

Coffee substitutes and other beverages made from wheat, rye or barley products: Postum, Ovaltine, malted drinks, soy milk with barley malt etc. (Check labels for ingredients).

Alcoholic and dealcoholized beverages: beer, ale, gin, whiskies, vodka, ethyl alcohol etc.

Breads

Black bread, chapatti, gluten-free, gluten, graham, matzo, nan, paratha, pita, pumpernickel, roti, sprouted wheat spelt, kamut or rye bread, steamed buns, whole wheat, white breads.

Corn, oat, potato, rice, rye, soy bean etc. breads all may contain wheat flour. Check labels carefully.

Cereals

Any cooked and cold cereals may contain wheat. This may include unexpected sources such as brands of corn flakes, multigrain cereals, oat and rice cereals.

Wheat may be modified and labelled as cous-cous, bulgur, semolina, cream of wheat. Triticale is a wheat/rye hybrid and should be avoided. Spelt, dinkle and kamut are close relatives of wheat and usually cross-react. Avoid cereals containing malt which is derived from barley. Tsampa is roasted barley. Read labels carefully.

Desserts

Cakes, candy bars, chocolate candy, commercial candies, cookies, custards, doughnuts, dumplings, filo pastry, ice creams, ice cream cones, pastries, pies, puddings made with wheat products, sherbets. Wheat may be used as a thickener in any dessert product.

Prepared mixes for cakes, cookies, ice creams, puddings and pie crusts, unless the list of ingredients shows no wheat products. Check labels carefully.

Flour

All-purpose, atta, bran, bread, bread crumbs, cake, cracked wheat, cracker meal, durum, enriched, entire wheat, farina, flour, gluten, gluten free, graham, malt, phosphated flour, pastry, roti, self-rising, semolina, wheat germ, wheat, white, whole flour, whole meal, whole wheat.

Any product labelled "flour" contains wheat.

Rye flour is usually cross-reactive with wheat and may be contaminated with up to 10% wheat flour during the milling process.

Barley is usually cross-reactive with wheat.

Malt

Malt is used as sweetener in a multitude of baked foods, candies, cereals, milk drinks, packaged foods, beverages etc. It is a product of barley.

Meats, Poultry, Game, Fish and Seafood

Bread and cracker stuffing, bologna, breaded meats, fish or vegetables, chili cold cuts, con carne, croquettes, deli meats, fish patties, hot dogs, hamburgers, lunch, canned and prepared meats, meat patties and loaves (unless made at home without wheat products, commercial and dealer-prepared meats frequently contain wheat products), salami, sausages, Swiss steak.

Miscellaneous

Alphabets, baking powder may contain wheat, caramel, dextrin, dumplings, farfel, gluten (fu), hydrolysed vegetable protein, kern, macaroni, malt products. MSG, noodles and pasta, ravioli, saitan, soup nuts and rings, spaghetti, tempura, vermicelli, vinegar. Corn is a British term for wheat.

Starch - usually refers to wheat or corn.

Salad Dressings

Any salad dressing thickened with wheat flour. White distilled vinegar is often made by the chemical breakdown of wood but it may be derived from wheat.

Sauces and Gravies

Bouillon cubes, butter sauces, cream and white sauces unless home made without wheat flour, gravies, soy sauce and tamari (some brands do not contain wheat). Read labels on commercial sauces.

Soups

Cream soups, unless you made them at home without wheat flour. Vegetable and meat soups, chowders and bisques if thickened with wheat products. Read labels carefully.

Note: When you buy packaged foods, read the labels carefully to be sure that the list of ingredients includes none of the above. If a package of food lacks a list of ingredients or when you eat away from home, if you are unsure about any food and accurate information cannot be secured, use an alternate choice about which there can be no doubt.

Wheat Alternatives

Most people think that wheat and flour are synonymous terms. However there are many forms of flour derived from other grains, seeds, beans and vegetables that can be used in baking and cooking. Most of these are well known in various traditional cuisines and more recipes and ideas can be found in ethnic and international cookbooks.

Bread

Instead of using bread to wrap up a sandwich filling, use leafy vegetables such as lettuce, cabbage or chard leaves to roll up the filling. Celery sticks, green peppers, avocado halves, scooped out tomato, zucchini or cucumber halves or mushroom caps can be stuffed with your usual sandwich fillings. If you use sliced meats use them to wrap up vegetables, cooked rice or other cooked grains. An inside out sandwich! Corn tortillas, rice wrappers or pancakes made without wheat can be used instead of bread to roll up fillings for sandwiches. Rice cakes, oat cakes, pappadums, rice crackers and crackers from the recipe section can support your favourite fillings. For breakfast, snacks or lunch spread nut butters or cheese on sliced apples, pears, carrots or any fruit or vegetable. A rice loaf that is very much like bread, but with a different texture, is available by mail from Ener-G Foods in Seattle or in natural food stores.

If you have been using bread with meals to fill up, use starchy vegetables with meals instead. You could use, beans, lentils, squash, Jerusalem artichoke, potato, corn, taro, beets, carrot, sweet potato, turnip, etc. Many of these are listed on the rotation diet chart on page 60. Wheat free muffins, crackers, pancakes or any of the items listed in the previous paragraph will help you to get enough to eat so that you do not lose weight. If you still feel hungry after a wheat free meal and only bread will satisfy that hunger, you may have a "food addiction". Also check that you are getting enough protein in your diet. Check the lists on page 53. Most people find that after avoiding wheat for several weeks that they will lose their bread craving .

Breading and Topping

Rice cakes or oat flakes can be ground in a blender and the crumbs used instead of wheat crumbs. Nuts or seeds can be ground and similarly used.

Cold Cereals

Use puffed rice, corn, oats or millet, granola or muesli but check for wheat. These can be found in supermarkets or health food stores.

Cooked Grains

Instead of bread or potatoes serve a cooked grain. For breakfast top with nuts, seeds or fruit. With lunch or dinner serve with vegetables, beans, meat or fish. See the recipes on page 154 for ideas on sauces to put on the cooked grains.

How to Cook Grains and Cereals

Add the grain to boiling water except for corn meal which should be added to cold water and stirred regularly. Turn down the heat and allow to simmer slowly. When the water is all absorbed the grain is ready to eat. If the grain has been in storage for some time it may require more water or longer time to cook. Buckwheat will be firmer if it is first roasted in a pan and mixed with a beaten egg as it roasts.

Grain (1 cup dry)	Water	Cooking Time
Amaranth	2 cups	15-20 min.
Brown Rice	2 cups	30-45 min.
Buckwheat/Kasha	1 cup	15-20 min.
Corn meal	4 cups	20-30 min.
Millet	3.5 cups	35-45 min.
Oats	2 cups	10-15 min.
Quinoa	2 cups	15-20 min.
Wild Rice	4 cups	40 min.

Flour

Wheat is not the only flour that you can use for baking. In fact there are flours not even made from grains; beans, seeds, nuts, starchy vegetables can be made into flours for baking.

Quinoa, amaranth and buckwheat are not members of the grain family either. Most of these flours are used in traditional diets and more recipes for them can be found in international cookbooks.

These alternative flours seldom cook exactly like wheat. They do not have the gluten found in wheat which gives it the texture, lightness and strength that we are accustomed to. These flours will produce results that are good to eat but heavier, more crumbly or stickier than wheat products. Grains, especially nonwheat grains, vary in coarseness of grind and dryness depending on the length of time since milling. All recipes may require slight alteration of the amount of liquid to suit your flour.

Not all flours are suitable for all situations. Rice and potato flour will make things lighter. Sweet rice flour, tapioca and arrowroot will make them bind together better. Rice, oat and buckwheat are more crumbly than wheat. Coconut, nut and seed flour can be sprinkled in the bottom of a pie plate and used as pie crusts.

Spelt is a grain very closely related to wheat that very few wheat sensitive people tolerate. If you want to try it, start with small amounts to check if it is safe for you. It can replace wheat cup for cup in any recipe calling for whole wheat flour.

If some of these flours are unavailable in stores near you, make your own. Grind oat flakes, unroasted buckwheat, nuts or seeds in a blender. Buckwheat flour made this way has a milder flavour than dark buckwheat flour that you purchase. If flours seem bitter, they may be old. If you can, grind your own with a hand cranked grain mill.

These flours are available from supermarkets, ethnic, specialty and natural food stores. Like any other whole food they may go bad with storage. If you use them infrequently store them in the refrigerator or freezer away from damp, warm areas and out of direct light.

How to Use Other Flours

Replace 1 cup wheat flour with:

Amaranth flour - 1 cup

Arrowroot flour - ½ cup - use as a thickener. Do not overcook.

Barley flour - ½ cup - not recommended with wheat allergy.

Buckwheat flour - 1 cup

Chickpea and other bean flours - ¾ cup

Corn flour - 1 cup - use as a thickener. Do not overcook.

Cornstarch - ½ cup + rye, potato or rice flour - ½ cup.

Millet flour - 1 cup

Oat flour - 1½ cups

Potato flour - ⅝ cup - combine with other flours for baking.

Quinoa flour - 1 cup

Rice flour - ¾ cup brown rice flour + ¼ sweet rice flour or ⅞ cup rice flour.

Rye flour - 1½ cups - not recommended with wheat allergy.

Soy flour - 1⅔ cups - soy should make up only 20% of the flour in a recipe.
      Bake at 25° less than the recipe calls for.

Tapioca flour - ½ cup - use for sauces, fruit fillings, glazes. Do not boil or
      overcook.

Noodles

There are many types of noodles now available not made with wheat. Rice noodles both fat and thin, flat and round; bean thread/starch noodles which become transparent with cooking; pure buckwheat (be careful as most buckwheat noodles contain wheat flour); corn spaghetti and macaroni; quinoa macaroni; sweet potato noodles. Spaghetti squash bakes into instant vegetable noodles. Some infants will like to eat hijiki or arame seaweeds instead of spaghetti. See the recipes for instructions on how to cook these. Use them with your usual spaghetti sauces or try the ones in the recipes.

Thickeners

See the list of thickeners in Egg Alternatives section on page 47.

Yeast, Malt and Mould Foods

Beverages

All alcoholic and fermented beverages: beer, brandy, gin, root beer, rum, vodka, whisky, wine, dealcoholized beverages etc.

Packaged fruit juices may contain traces of mould. Boxed juices are most likely to have mould residues. Only juices that you squeeze at home from mould free fruit are completely mould free. Juices are probably a minor source.

Bread

All raised bread (except some baking soda breads), hamburger buns, hot dog buns, pita, rolls, raised doughs, etc. Frozen biscuits, breads, buns, rolls etc. Sprouted wheat and sourdough breads use a naturally occurring yeast. Avoid them too. Breads without yeast are usually heavy and flat.

Cheese

Cheeses made with mould such as blue, Gorgonzola, etc. Most other cheeses are mould free, except for surface contamination or if spoiled.

Condiments and Sauces

Vinegars such as apple, pear, grape and wine. These may appear in such foods as: barbecue sauce, condiments, French dressing, horseradish, ketchup, Marmite, mayonnaise, olives, pickles, salad dressing, sauerkraut, soya sauce, tomato sauce, Vegemite etc. Black pepper often contains aspergillus mould. Miso, tempeh, tamari, soya sauce and other fermented soy products. These are made using aspergillus, a mould. White distilled vinegar is manufactured using either a chemical process or a bacterium, Acetobactor aceti.

Jams and sauces without preservatives may quickly grow mould on the surface.

Fungal Foods

Mushrooms, truffles, morels, fungus.

Leftovers

All foods may develop surface mould after exposure to air. This is especially true of cheese and ground meat. Remove a thin layer from the cheese before eating. Meat can be ground as you wait at the butcher's and should be cooked without delay. Leftovers should be cooled quickly, frozen if possible and eaten soon.

Meat, Fish and Poultry

Meat, fish and poultry when cooked in bread or cracker crumbs. Sausages, pepperoni, salami, mortadella etc.

Nutritional Yeast

Brewer's yeast, torula yeast, engevita yeast, etc.

Pastries

Cookies, crackers, pretzels, cakes and cake mixes etc.

Processed Foods

Some foods acquire mould growths during preparation, processing or after exposure to air, even when refrigerated, such as ham, bacon, preserves, jams, jellies, syrups, canned fruit and vegetables, baked items, molasses, cheeses, dairy products. Leavening is a term often used for baker's yeast.

Vitamins

Vitamins may contain yeast. Check the labels before taking them.
B vitamins and multivitamin preparations are most likely to contain yeast.

Milk Foods

Baked Goods
Any bakery item may contain milk. Baking powder biscuits, biscuits, breads, cakes, cookies, doughnuts, hot cakes, muffins, pancakes, pie crust, popovers, soda crackers, waffles, Zwieback.

Beverages
Cocoa drinks, malted milk, Ovaltine, smoothies, sodas.

Dairy Products
Butter, buttermilk, canned milks, cheese, cream, curd, dried milk, goat's milk, kefir, ice cream, malted milk, milk, panir, powdered milk, sour cream, whey, whipping cream, yogurt, most margarine. Although all cheeses are milk products, some people not sensitive to milk may be found allergic to one or more cheeses.

Desserts and Sweets
Blanc mange, candies, candy bars, caramel, chocolate, creme caramel, custard, ice cream, junket, mousse, nougat, pudding, sherbet.

Eggs Dishes
Scrambled eggs, souffles.

Meats and Vegetables
"Au gratin" foods, bologna, butter fried foods, creamed foods, fritters, hamburgers, hash, hot dogs and other sausages (skim milk is used as a binder), mashed potatoes, meat loaf, wiener schnitzel.

Sauces and Dressings
Cream sauces, gravies, hard sauces, some salad dressings (check labels), butter sauces.

Soups
Bisques, chowders, cream soups

Other

Casein, caseinate, popcorn with butter, rarebit, lactose. Non-dairy creamers may contain caseinate. Powdered artificial sweeteners may contain lactose. Margarine may contain the milk solid casein. Soy cheese may contain casein or whey.

Milk Alternatives

Milk

Nut, soy, rice and seed milks can be used in baking or on cereals instead of cow milk. Juice can also be used instead of milk in recipes and on cereals. None of these alternatives will have the calcium content of cow milk. Because 70% of people allergic to cow milk will also react to goat milk, it is not a recommended substitute. See page 65 for nut milk and juice recipes. Soy and rice milks are available in natural food stores.

Cheese

For a nutritious snack, nuts (perhaps mixed with dried fruit) can be used instead of cheese. Nut butters can be used as a spread instead of cheese slices. Crumble firm tofu onto a salad instead of cheese bits.

Butter

Soy lecithin spread is available from health food stores. Use nut butters as a spread. In cooking, fry with vegetable oils such as olive, sunflower or peanut oil. Dip or spread good quality olive oil on bread.

Yogurt

See the recipe for tofu yogurt on page 180. Cultured soy yogurt is available in health food stores.

Egg Foods

Baked Goods
Baking powder may contain egg (check the label). Bisquick, cake flour, cakes, cookies, diet cookies, doughnuts, meringues, French toast. fritters, frostings, glazed bread and rolls, krupek (shrimp crackers), macaroons, muffins, pancakes, pastry, pie crust, pretzels, waffles.

Beverages
Coffee, egg nog, malted drinks, Ovaltine, ovamalt, root beer, wine (many are cleared with egg white)

Dessert and Candy
Chocolate bars, chocolate, cream pies, custard, marshmallow, nougat, ice cream, puddings, sherbet, soft candies.

Egg Products
Dried egg powder, egg noodles, omelets, raw and cooked eggs, souffles.

Meats, Vegetables and Soups
Batters for frying, breaded foods, fritters, hamburger, luncheon meats, meat jellies, meat loaf, packaged meats, patties, potato salad, sausages. Noodle and consomme soups.

Sauces and Dressings
Boiled dressings, Caesar salad, hollandaise, mayonnaise, salad dressings, tartar sauce.

Skin Contacts
Vaginal suppositories, eye drops, nasal sprays containing lysozyme.

Other names for Egg
Albumin, conalbumin, globulin, livetin, mucoid, ovomucoid, ovalbumin, ovovitellin, vitellin and yolk. Commercial egg replacers may contain egg. Chicken eggs usually cross-react with eggs from other birds; avoid them too.

Egg Alternatives

Eggs are used in recipes to bind the ingredients, to thicken or to leaven, that is to raise and lighten. Usually eggs can be replaced by an appropriate alternative listed below.

Binders
Each is equivalent to one egg.
1. Soft tofu - ¼ cup.
2. Flaxseed - 1 Tbs. boiled in 1 cup water for 15 minutes. Add to muffins.
3. Psyllium seed husk - 1 Tbs. with 3 Tbs. water and let sit briefly.
4. Gelatin powder - 1 tsp. softened in 3 Tbs. boiling water. Stir until dissolved. When thickened beat until frothy.
5. Arrowroot powder - 1 tsp. will hold together meats, beans etc. in patties and loaves.

Leavening
1. 1 tsp. baking powder for each egg substituted for leavening.
2. 1 tsp. vinegar (if tolerated) for each egg in a cake recipe.

Thickeners
1. Cornstarch - 1 Tbs. thickens 1½ cups liquid.
2. Arrowroot - 2½ tsp. thickens 1 cup liquid. Use within 10 minutes of cooking. Do not reheat.
3. Tapioca - 3 tsp. thickens 1 cup liquid. Do not boil or over cook.
4. Potato flour or starch - 2½ tsp. thickens 1 cup liquid. Do not allow to boil.
5. Agar agar - 1 tsp. will thicken 1 cup of liquid. Do not boil too long.
6. Chickpea flour - 1 Tbs. for 1 cup. This is traditionally used to thicken curries.

Commercial egg replacer usually contains potato starch, tapioca flour, and baking powder. If used as a dry powder, add more water to recipe. Use for leavening or as a binder. Check labels, some may contain egg.

Corn Foods

Baked Goods

Baking powder (check label), Bisquick, breads and pastries (check with baker), corn breads, frostings, icings, Indian pudding, pies, pumpernickel, tortillas.

Beverages

Ales, beers, hard liquors, lagers, soft drinks, sparkling wine, except good imported wines and brandy, wine

Corn Products

Breakfast cereals. corn flakes, corn chips, corn noodles, corn syrup, corn flour, corn oil (Mazola), corn starch, dextrin, dextrose, fresh, frozen or canned corn, fritters, glucose, grits, hominy, invert sugar, mannitol, popped corn, sorbitol, succotash, sugar. Maize is the British term for corn.

Desserts and Candy

Canned fruits, caramels, chocolates, cough drops, custard, hard candies, ice cream, jam, jelly, malted foods, preserves, pudding.

Meats and Vegetables

Bacon, batters for frying, canned soup, cold meats, deli meats, ham, hot dog, luncheon meats, pickles, processed cheese, sauerkraut, sausage.

Sauces and Dressings

Acetic acid, corn oil (Mazola), deep fried foods, gravies, margarine, salad dressings, thickened sauces, white vinegar, white sauce. Sauces on Chinese food are usually thickened with corn starch.

Other

Tablets and capsules may contain corn starch. Adhesives. Laundry starch. Many products such as paper cups, plastic bags and container are dusted with corn starch to prevent sticking.

Soy Bean Foods

Baked Goods
Breads, cakes, packaged mixes, pastries, rolls (check with baker). Roasted soy nuts are often used to replace peanuts.

Beverages
Soy milk/drink, coffee substitutes (check label), protein drinks. Prosobee Isomil, Soyalac

Cereals
Soy flakes, boxed breakfast cereals (check label), soy noodles.

Cheese
Processed cheese, soy cheese.

Desserts and Candy
Caramel, chocolate, hard candy, ice cream, nut candy, sherbet.

Meats and Vegetables
Bean curd, cold cuts, deli meats, hamburger, hamburger extender, hot dogs, meat loaf, natto, sausage, soy bean sprouts, soy grits, tofu, TVP (texturized vegetable protein), vegetable protein.

Sauces, Dressings and Oils
Mayonnaise, salad dressings and vegetable oils may contain soy oil. Crisco, lecithin spread, margarine, miso, soy sauce, tamari, Worcestershire and similar sauces

Other names for soy
Lecithin, emulsifiers, TVP are often derived from soy.

Sugar Foods

Sugar and concentrated sweeteners may have any of a large variety of different names depending on the source and chemical structure of the sweetener: barley malt, beet sugar, cane sugar, caramel, carob syrup, corn syrup, corn sugar, date sugar, dextrose, fructose, glucose. golden syrup, gur, honey, invert sugar, jaggery, lactose, maltose, malt, maple syrup, molasses, palm sugar, pancake syrup, praline, rice syrup, sorbitol, xylitol.

Sugar Alternatives

Most people with food allergies feel better when they avoid sugars and sweeteners. This may be due to an allergy to the sweetener or because of the metabolic effect of the sugar. All concentrated and refined sugars have virtually the same metabolic effect on your body. The sweeteners listed below will work well in place of sugar in some recipes but not in all. If you use a liquid sweetener you may need to reduce the amount of fluid or increase the flour in a recipe. You could also add extra chopped fruit to a recipe to add sweetness.

In these and most recipes, the sweetener could be left out entirely. The recipe will not be as sweet but usually will otherwise work. If you do not wish to totally remove the sugar from a recipe, it can usually be cut down to a ¼ of that suggested in most other cookbooks without harming the recipe.

Substitute for 1 cup sugar		Reduction of total liquid
Barley Malt	1 cup	⅓ cup
Date Sugar	1 cup	nil
Date Jam (page 188)	1½ cups	¼ cup
Fruit Juice	1 cup	1 cup
Honey, Rice Syrup	¼ cup	⅛ cup
Maple Syrup	¾ cup	⅛ cup
Prune Spread (page 189)	¾ cup	⅛ cup
Raisin Jam (page 187)	¾ cup	⅛ cup
Molasses	¾ cup	⅛ cup

Staying Well Nourished

One of the most challenging and important aspects of controlling food allergy reactions is staying well nourished while avoiding food allergens. Because children are still growing, it is essential that they get enough protein, carbohydrate, oils/fats, vitamins and minerals to maintain that growth. If you use whole foods and keep your child away from junk food and excessive concentrated sweeteners your child will eventually learn to eat a wide variety of different nutritious foods and grow to his or her optimum level. In the initial stages of an avoidance diet when the number of foods that you or your child eat is restricted, helping yourself to stay well nourished will require your close attention. Later, when you are able to re-introduce more foods and you or your child is eating a diversified diet this will be much easier.

The nutrients that are often most to difficult to provide on an avoidance diet are protein, and calcium. These and others are discussed on the following pages. If you are avoiding several foods, taking a good multiple vitamin and multiple mineral will help to insure that you are getting adequate amounts of these micro-nutrients.

Plan your meals in advance so that you have the food that you will need on hand when you want it. Discuss your diet with your housemates. Ask for their support and encouragement. An adult can expect a five pound weight loss initially. This usually returns when you have adapted to your new eating pattern. Unless you are overweight, do not let your weight drop further without speaking to your doctor. The weight loss is usually caused by not eating enough new foods to replace the ones that you are avoiding.

Mark your favourite recipes and any changes you make to them. Record new recipes or adaptations of the recipes. It is often useful during the first few weeks to record everything that you eat and how you feel during the day.

You are working on feeling better by effectively using this eating plan and although it would be a mistake to attribute every untoward event in your life to allergy, isn't it nice to be gaining a sense of control over your health.

Protein Requirements

The groups most at risk for inadequate protein intake in North American are vegetarians and those avoiding multiple foods. It is essential that you insure an adequate protein intake. The table on page 56 indicates the amount of protein needed at different ages and the table on the next page the amount of protein to be found in foods. You will notice that vegetables are not a good source of protein. Fruits are not listed since they do not contain significant amounts of protein. There is also a table with which you can determine your daily minimum protein requirement. It is useful to calculate your average daily protein intake over a period of a week. Do this after you have been on your avoidance diet for a week or two. If you are not eating enough protein and you cannot think of ways to increase the amount of protein in your diet, you should speak to your doctor or a dietician.

Protein is an essential nutrient for both children and adults. Proteins are themselves made up of amino acids. There are twenty-two amino acids that the body uses to make up proteins. Of these eight must be supplied by food. Proteins are the major components of muscle and all other tissues and cells of the body. All of the chemical processes of the body are reliant on enzymes which are types of proteins. Many of the hormones and chemical messengers of the body are proteins or amino acids. Proteins can also be used as a source of energy when there is not enough fat or carbohydrate in the diet. Protein deficiency can cause weakness, fatigue, fluid retention, muscle loss, bone fragility, reduced organ function and in children slowing of growth and mental dullness. Insufficient protein intake may also lead to anemia and problems with blood sugar metabolism.

Persons who are doing heavy work or who are ill with an infection will need to increase this amount by 25%. For example, a thirty year old male doing heavy work requires 57 grams x 1¼ = 70 grams of protein daily.

Protein Content of Foods in Grams

Legumes (1 cup cooked)

Black beans	12
Garbanzo	13
Kidney beans	16
Lentils	12
Lima beans	10
Mung beans	12
Navy Beans	15
Peas	21
Soy milk	9
Soy	17
Tofu, 3½ ounces	8
White beans	15

Nuts and Seeds (1 oz)

Almonds	5
Brazil nuts	4
Cashews	5
Chestnuts	1
Hazelnuts/filberts	3
Peanuts	8
Pumpkin seeds	8
Sesame seeds	5
Sunflower seeds	7
Walnuts	6

Vegetables (1 cup cooked)

Alfalfa sprouts, 1 oz.	1.5
Broccoli, 1 stalk	6
Brussels sprouts	7
Cauliflower	3
Corn, 1 ear	4
Green peas	10
Mung bean sprouts	4
Potato, one medium	4
Spinach	3
Squash	4

Seafood (100 g. or 3½ oz.)

Clams	14
Cod	18
Crab	17
Halibut	21
Salmon	20
Scallops	15
Squid	16
Tuna Canned	24

Meats and Poultry
(100 g. or 3½ oz. serving)

Chicken	23
Egg-one	6
Hamburger	25
Lamb	20
Lean steak	25
Pork	29
Turkey	31

Grains (1⅓ cup uncooked)

Barley	6
Bread whole wheat, 1 slice	2.4
Light buckwheat flour	9
Millet	6
Oatmeal	4
Rice	5
Wheat	8

Dairy

Cheddar cheese, 1 oz.	7
Cottage cheese, dry 1 cup	25
Milk solids, 1 oz.	10
Milk, 1 cup	9
Parmesan cheese, 1 oz.	10
Swiss cheese, 1 oz.	8
Yogurt, 1 cup	8

Calcium Requirements

The following page is a list of calcium containing foods and on page 56 is a table to help you determine your daily calcium needs. Food groups not listed, such as grains do not contain significant amounts of calcium. You should first calculate your average daily calcium intake over a period of one week. If you are not getting enough calcium, then either increase the amount of calcium containing foods you eat or take a calcium supplement. Up to 60% of the population may not be eating enough calcium. It is especially common for women not to get sufficient calcium in their diets.

Calcium is essential for the production and maintenance of bones and the proper function of nerves and muscles. Vitamin D, derived from sun exposure, enriched food (usually dairy products) or supplements is necessary for calcium absorbtion. People who are not frequently exposed to direct sunlight such as seniors or those who work indoors through the daylight hours could take 100-200 IU of Vitamin D daily. Calcium deficiency can cause muscle spasms, tics and defective nerve function. Particularly for women a lifetime deficiency in calcium intake can lead to the development of osteoporosis after menopause with an increased risk of bone fractures.

If dairy products are avoided, getting enough calcium from food alone is very difficult. In that situation a calcium supplement is usually necessary. Most types of calcium supplements will be absorbed by the bowel in approximately equal amounts. However some brands of calcium pills may be too hard to dissolve before passing out of the bowel. If digestion problems are suspected then calcium in powdered, liquid, capsule or chewable form is best. Avoid tablets or liquids with colouring or sugar. The powder or liquid could be mixed with food or beverages. Effervescent tablets are available that will make a fizzy drink when added to water or added to juice.

Low stomach acid production can reduce calcium absorption. People with low stomach acid will absorb calcium best when it is taken with food. Generally calcium is best absorbed when taken with dinner.

Most natural calcium pills, such as dolomite, oyster shell and bone meal, have been found to have excessive levels of lead contamination. Using calcium carbonate or calcium citrate not from natural sources may be best, especially for children. Because calcium interferes with the absorption of other minerals it is best to take it by itself and take other minerals at another time.

Calcium Content of Foods in Milligrams

Fish (3½ oz.)

Cod	29
Halibut	20
Herring - canned	147
Oyster	85
Red Snapper	16
Salmon	175
Sardine - canned	303
Shrimp	63
Trout	45
Tuna - canned	9

Dairy

Cheddar (1 oz.)	200
Gouda (1 oz.)	200
Mozzarella(1 oz.)	163
Parmesan (1 oz.)	329
Ricotta 1 cup	509
Milk 1 cup	291
Yogurt 1 cup	274

Seaweeds (100 grams)

Dulse	567
Hijiki	1400
Kelp - 1 Tbs.	156
Kombu	800
Nori	260

Fruit

Apricot - 3 medium	15
Dates - 10	27
Pear - 1 medium	19
Raisin - ½ cup	54

Vegetables (1 cup)

Beet greens cooked	198
Black beans dry	270
Broccoli cooked	136
Carrots cooked	51
Chickpeas cooked	106
Chinese cabbage	52
Collards cooked	220
Green beans	67
Kale cooked	206
Kidney beans cooked	70
Parsley raw	122
Pinto beans	257
Soy milk	55
Soy sprouts	50
Soy beans cooked	131
Spinach cooked	176
Torula yeast 1 oz.	120
Turnip cooked	54

Nuts

Almonds (12-15)	38
Brazil nuts (4)	28
Hazelnuts (10-12)	38
Peanuts, raw (1 oz)	13
Sesame seeds (1 oz)	35
Sunflower seeds (1 oz)	34

Meats

Chicken ¼ lb.	7
Egg	127
Ground beef, lean ¼ lb	14
Lamb ¼ lb.	10
Liver ¼ lb.	2

Recommended Nutrient Intakes

Age	Sex	Calcium	Protein
Months		mg/day	g/day
0-6	Both	400	13
7-12	Both	600	17
Years			
1-3	Both	800	19
4-6	Both	800	25
7-10	Both	800	31
11-14	M	1200	43
	F	1200	41
15-18	M	1200	54
	F	1200	47
19-24	M	1200	57
	F	1200	41
25-50	M	800	57
	F	800	41
51+	M	800	57
	F	1200	41
Pregnancy		1300	additional 20
Breast Feeding		1300	additional 20

Fibre

Dietary fibre is often ignored as an essential daily nutrient. If you are not eating enough fibre you are likely to become constipated. You can avoid this by using whole grains and raw fruits and vegetables every day. If you still have problems with bowel movements then you could use the following fibre sources. In addition to helping regular, easy bowel movements, fibre plays a role in lowering cholesterol levels and reducing the risk of bowel cancer.

DAY ONE

On Day One of the rotation you can use psyllium seed husk powder, available from health food stores. Start with ½ teaspoon, two times daily. Mix it into a glass of cool water or juice. Drink the mixture quickly before it gels. Follow that by drinking a second glass of water or juice. Increase the amount used up to one tablespoon, twice daily. The amount required will depend on the size of the person and the amount of fibre in the rest of the diet.

DAY TWO

Use from one teaspoon up to one tablespoon of flax seeds. You could let them sit for several hours in a glass of water and then drink the thick fluid that develops or grind the seeds in a blender or coffee mill. Sprinkle the ground flax seeds on cereal or mix them with water or juice. Drink the seeds using two glasses of water as with the psyllium. The flax seeds should be ground freshly every day as they will quickly go rancid after grinding

DAY THREE

Sprinkle rice bran onto your food as you would wheat bran or mix from 1 tsp. to ¼ cup with water and spoon or drink the mixture.

DAYFOUR

Use oat bran. Cook up one half cup of oat bran with one cup of water as you would porridge. It cooks in 3 minutes.

Food Sources of Vitamins and Minerals

These food sources of vitamins and minerals are listed in descending order of concentration of the specific nutrient. That is, if eaten in the same weight, the first listed food will have more of the nutrient than the second and so on.

Calcium - see page 55

Copper - oyster, nuts, whole grains, dry peas, beef liver, peanuts, lamb, sunflower oil.

Chromium - brewer's yeast, calf's liver, beef, whole grains, oysters, potatoes.

Iodine - clams, shrimp, haddock, halibut, oysters, salmon, sardines, beef liver, pineapple.

Iron - kelp, brewer's yeast, pumpkin seeds, beef liver, sunflower seeds, millet, parsley, clams, nuts, dried prunes, beef, raisins, dark green leafy vegetables

Magnesium - kelp, nuts, brewer's yeast, whole grains, tofu, green leafy vegetables, soy beans.

Manganese - nuts, whole grains, dried peas, green leafy vegetables, carrots, broccoli.

Molybdenum - lentils, beef liver, dry peas, cauliflower, green peas, brewer's yeast.

Nickel - canned foods, soy beans, beans, lentils, peas, nuts, whole grains, parsley.

Phosphorus - pumpkin and sunflower seeds, soy bean, cheese, nuts.

Potassium - seaweed, sunflower seeds, nuts, raisins, peanuts, dates, figs, avocado, yams, green leafy vegetables, potatoes with skins, bananas, carrots.

Selenium - tuna, herring, smelt, Brazil nuts, shellfish, whole grains, liver.

Vanadium - buckwheat, parsley, unrefined vegetable oils, soy bean, egg, oat, corn.

Zinc - oyster, beefsteak, lamb, nuts, dried peas, beef liver, milk, egg yolk, whole grains.

Vitamin A - liver, egg yolk, dark green leafy vegetables, deep yellow vegetables, tomatoes, butter, whole milk, cheese.

Vitamin D - halibut liver oil, cod liver oil, fresh mackerel, sardines, herring, salmon, tuna, egg yolk, shrimp, liver, butter.

Vitamin E - soy oil, corn oil, peanut oil, sweet potatoes, navy beans, brown rice, turnip greens, green peas, whole eggs, butter, oatmeal, liver.

Thiamine (B_1) - sunflower seeds, pork, liver, yeast, lean meats, eggs, green leafy vegetables, whole grains, berries, nuts, legumes.

Riboflavin (B_2) - liver, milk, cheese meat, eggs, green leafy vegetables, whole grains, legumes, sesame seeds.

Niacin (B_3) - liver, meats, fish, sunflower seeds, whole grains, dry peas and beans, nuts, peanut butter.

Pyridoxine (B_6) - sunflower seeds, wheat germ, calf liver, meats, whole grains, fish, soy beans, peanuts, yams, tuna, tomatoes, corn, carrots.

Biotin - liver, peanuts, egg yolk, nuts, cauliflower, mushrooms, dry peas, lima beans.

Pantothenic Acid - liver, dark green leafy vegetables, asparagus, lima beans, kidney, nuts, whole grains, bran, meats, mushrooms, dry peas, soy beans, salmon.

Folic Acid - liver, dark green leafy vegetables, asparagus, lima beans, kidney, nuts, whole grains, lentils.

Vitamin B_{12} - clams, liver, kidney, beef, sole, scallops, haddock. Poor sources: milk, cheese, egg. No B_{12} content: fruit, vegetables.

Vitamin C - citrus fruits, strawberries, cantaloupe, uncooked vegetables especially pepper, broccoli, cauliflower, kale, brussels sprouts, turnip greens, cabbage, tomatoes, potatoes. Especially sensitive to losses from heating, cutting of foods, and poor ripening.

Bioflavonoids - grapes, rosehips, prunes, citrus (especially white parts), cherry, plum, parsley.

Four Day Rotary Diversified Diet Plan

DAY ONE

FISH
60. Grouper, Sea Bass
80. Sturgeon
81. Shark
82. Anchovy
83. Salmon, Trout, Char, Steelhead
84. Lake Whitefish

MEAT & SHELLFISH
58. Mollusks: Clam, Abalone, Mussel, Squid, Octopus
63. Beef, Veal, Goat, Buffalo, Cow & Goat cheese, Gelatin

BEVERAGES
9. Coffee
13. Dandelion & Chicory coffee, Chamomile tea
14. Carob, Fenugreek
33. Pineapple juice
63. Cow milk, Goat milk

VEGETABLES
13. Lettuce, Dandelion, Artichoke
14. Alfalfa sprouts, Bean sprouts
16. Zucchini, Cucumber
48. Hops
56. Mushroom, Fungus
75. New Zealand Spinach

DAY TWO

85. Smelt
86. Pike
87. Carp
88. Catfish
89. Cod, Hake, Haddock, Pollack
90. Mullet

61. Duck, Goose
62. Chicken, Quail, Pheasant, Turkey, Squab (Pigeon), Dove, Guinea Fowl, Partridge, Egg

12. Tomato juice
34. Papaya juice
35. Grape juice
37. Mint Tea

7. Nopales (Cactus)
12. Tomato, Eggplant, Peppers, Tomatillo
17. Asparagus, Onion, Chives, Leeks, Garlic
57. Nasturtium
77. Dulse, Kelp, Arame, Hijiki, Nori

DAY THREE

91. Eel
92. Grouper, Black Bass
93. Herring, Sardine, Shad, Menhaden, Kippers
94. Red Snapper
95. Yellow Perch, Pike
96. Bluefish

59. Crustaceans: Crab, Shrimp, Lobster, Crayfish
65. Lamb
65. Sheep cheese

30. Wintergreen tea, Cranberry juice
32. Orange, Lemon and Grapefruit juice

18. Spinach, Chard, Lamb's quarters
19. Parsley, Celery, Fennel, Coriander
73. Capers
39. Fiddlehead Fern

DAY FOUR

97. Amberjack, Pompano
98. Porgy
99. Mackerel, Tuna, Bonita
100. Mahi Mahi
101. Flounder, Halibut
102. Sole
103. Ocean Perch, Roughy

66. Pork
68. Rabbit
67. Venison: Moose, Deer, Cariboo

26. Apple juice, Pear juice
27. Rosehip tea, Prune juice, Apricot
38. Ginger tea
43. Green tea, Black tea
45. Jamaica (Hibiscus)

15. Cabbage, Radish, Cauliflower, Kale, Brussel Sprouts, Broccoli, Collard, Chinese Cabbage, Watercress, Mustard, Arugula
29. Olive
36. Grape Leaves
45. Okra

STARCHY VEGETABLES

13. Jerusalem Artichoke, Burdock (Gobo)
14. Dried Beans, Peas, Green Beans, Lentils, Dal, Soy Bean, Jicama
16. Squash, Pumpkin
25. Plantain

4. Corn
10. Taro (Poi, Dasheen), Malanga
12. Potato
28. Avocado
70. Lotus Root

8. Cassava, Yuca
18. Beets
19. Carrots, Parsnip, Fennel
79. Water Chestnuts

2. Bamboo Shoots
15. Turnip
20. Sweet Potato
74. Yam

FRUIT

14. Tamarind, Carob pod
16. Pumpkin, Cantaloupe, Melon, Watermelon
25. Banana
33. Pineapple
48. Fig, Mulberry, Jackfruit, Breadfruit
54. Mango
64. Durian

7. Prickly Pear (Tuna, Sabra)
23. Persimmon
24. Raspberry, Strawberry, Blackberry
34. Papaya
35. Grape, Raisins
40. Passion Fruit (Granadilla)
41. Custard Apple, Cherimoya
42. Paw-paw

21. Kiwi Fruit
30. Blueberry, Cranberry
32. Orange, Pomelo, Lemon, Lime, Grapefruit, Tangerine
50. Date, Sago, Coconut
69. Mangosteen
71. Litchi, Longan, Rambutan
111. Starfruit (Carambola)
112. Sapodilla, Sapota

11. Rhubarb
26. Apple, Pear, Quince, Loquat,
27. Prune, Plum, Apricot, Cherry
27. Peach
31. Currant, Gooseberry
32. Pomegranate
36. Guava
58. Rosehips

FLOURS and GRAINS

1. Wheat, Spelt, Bran, Rye, Barley
13. Psyllium
14. Chickpea, Soy, Lentil, Peanut
14. Carob flour
56. Brewer's Yeast

12. Potato Flour
4. Millet, Corn, Sorghum
70. Lotus Root Flour
77. Agar Agar
110. Teff

3. Wild Rice
6. Rice, Rice Bran
8. Tapioca, Yuca, Cassava
18. Amaranth, Quinoa

11. Buckwheat
5. Oat, Oat Bran
9. Arrowroot

SEEDS and NUTS

13. Sunflower Seeds
14. Peanuts
16. Pumpkin seeds (Pepitas)
52. Poppy Seeds

44. Sesame Seeds
46. Flax Seeds
53. Walnut, Pecan

47. Filbert, Hazelnut
76. Pine Nut

27. Almond
51. Brazil Nut
55. Chestnut
72. Macadamia Nut

SWEETS

1. Barley Malt
14. Carob Syrup
41. & 57. Clover Honey

4. Molasses, Corn sugar - dextrose, glucose
6. Rice Syrup

50. Date Sugar

7. Pekmez (Grape syrup)
22. Pomegranate syrup (grenadine)
49. Maple Syrup

Introduction to Recipes

This recipe section contains easy, quick and good tasting recipes to help you control food allergy. Some use foods that may be new to you or use familiar foods in new ways. Let yourself be curious and experiment with them. You will find some new and exciting things to eat.

The recipes that follow are organized to follow the Rotary Diversified Diet also called the Rotation Diet or Rotation Plan. Most of the recipes are listed under headings of DAY ONE, DAY TWO, DAY THREE or DAY FOUR. These recipes contain only foods that fall on the appropriate days of the Rotation Diet. Recipes under NON-ROTATING RECIPES do not contain wheat, yeast or milk products but do not follow the Rotation Diet plan.

The flours that you purchase made from less commonly used grains, nuts and seeds may vary in moisture content, fineness of grind and age. Therefore you may need to slightly alter the amount of liquid that is needed in a recipe, either more or less depending on the quality of the flour.

If you or your family are sensitive to any ingredient in a recipe, try to substitute it with something else that is similar but tolerated. See the lists of wheat, milk and egg substitutes for ideas. If you use buckwheat flour, you will find that it has a milder taste if you buy unroasted buckwheat groats and grind them yourself in a grain mill or blender to make a light buckwheat flour.

If you are corn or wheat sensitive, you may want to avoid commercial baking soda which often contains these grains. You can make you own baking powder by mixing the ingredients listed below. They can all be obtained from your drug store.

Baking Powder

2 parts cream of tarter
1 part sodium or potassium bicarbonate

Mix all these very well and store in an air-tight container. When using this baking powder have the oven preheated and everything mixed in advance. When liquid is added to the powder it will act very quickly and dough will not stay light unless heated very quickly. This baking powder will not keep for long so make in small batches. To test if it is still working, add 1 teaspoon to a cup of water. It should bubble vigorously.

None of the recipes use sugar, honey or other concentrated sweeteners. If you or your child are clearly not reactive to sugar, you may want to use it in a recipe. You can either add extra sugar or substitute sugar for the dried fruit in the recipe. Salt is generally avoided in these recipes. If you prefer to use salt you can add a small amount.

The baked items that you make with these recipes will not taste or look exactly like things that you have made with wheat flour and milk. Because of its gluten content wheat is able to rise and hold together better than other flours. Do not label your baking a failure if it does not look or taste like things that you are accustomed to baking. You will find that you will become used to the new textures and tastes and may come to prefer them to wheat.

Many people find it very useful to record everything that they eat and how they feel each day during the first few weeks of starting the new diet. You may be able to discover other foods that bother you.

Do not give up. Don't lose heart if changes seem difficult at first. Everyone finds that they make mistakes and have problems at first when beginning a new type of eating plan. You will find after a few weeks that these changes will become easy to do, effortless and uncomplicated for you and your family.

Infant Meals

Your baby's tastes may be very different than yours so try a wide variety of new and different foods. Start with mashed foods and gradually increase the texture as baby learns to chew and teeth appear.

Fruit

Mashed banana
Apple sauce - steam apple pieces until very soft and then puree. Do not add sugar.
Pear, peach - steam chunks until soft. Serve when cool.
Papaya - mash or serve soft pieces.

Vegetables

Steam vegetables until soft. Mash and serve. Try squash, broccoli, potato, carrot, sweet potato, turnip, spinach, peas. You can add a little breast milk or formula to soften them.

Grains and Lentils

Baby cereals of individual grains can be cooked and a little breast milk or formula added. Red lentils will cook into a very soft porridge. Clean them thoroughly to remove any pebbles first.

Fish

Cook the fish until it flakes easily and is no longer translucent. Cool and break into small pieces. Very carefully feel each piece for bones before serving. Mash or serve in small pieces.

Beverages

You may have been asked to avoid favourite juices as well as soda pop, coffee and tea. You may be wondering what is left to drink. Water, in its many forms, is an ideal beverage. If not accustomed to drinking water, you could explore the use of carbonated mineral waters or club soda initially. Very cold water can be refreshing. Taken hot after boiling, with or without a twist of lemon, it can be as soothing as a cup of tea or coffee, especially in the morning, after meals or on cold days. Herbal teas, or tissanes, are available in a great variety of flavours. Do not confuse flavoured black tea with herbal teas. If you have a juicer, make your own fruit and vegetable juices. Some juices can be made in a blender by pressing and filtering the pulp after blending. This often works well after cooking the fruit.

DAY ONE

Shakes or Smoothies

These tasty and filling drinks can be made by combining any nut or seed milk with fresh or frozen fruit in a blender. Let your imagination and allergies determine the combinations.

Banana Carob Milkshake

¼ cup cashew nuts (optional)
1 tsp. carob powder
1 drop vanilla (optional)
1 ripe banana

1 tsp. honey or carob syrup
  (optional)
1 cup soy milk or water

Blend 1 minute until smooth. Omit carob for plain banana milkshake.

Peanut Banana Shake

1 cup milk: soy, seed or nut
3 Tbs. carob powder
1 2 tsp. honey or carob syrup
  (optional)

1 ripe banana
¼ cup smooth peanut or
  cashew butter

Blend all ingredients and enjoy!

Hot Carob

4 cups milk: cashew, coconut
  or soy
1 Tbs. honey or maple syrup
  (optional)

½ tsp. vanilla
2 Tbs. oil
3 Tbs. carob powder

Blend ingredients until smooth. Slowly add oil and blend together.
Heat if desired but do not boil.

Watermelon Juice

Watermelon and all melons make a cooling refreshing juice that is
wonderful on a hot day. If you have a juicer just slice the rind off
of a piece of watermelon. It is very juicy so you don't need much.
If you don't have a juicer blend the melon and then strain off the
juice. It is also very good combined half and half with sparkling
water.

Pineapple Juice Spritzer

1 litre pineapple juice
1 banana, thinly sliced
½ melon, thinly sliced

3 cups sparkling water
12 ice cubes

In a pitcher, or a bowl for a party, mix the juice and fruit slices. Stir
in the sparkling water and the ice cubes just before serving.

Soy Milk

You can buy soy milk at most supermarkets, health food stores and Asian grocery stores. You will find that different brands will have differing tastes. Try several until you find the one you like the best. Some brands come with barley malt or other sweeteners. If you are allergic to wheat or yeast avoid these. If fresh soy milk is not available, look for soy milk powder. Add water to reconstitute. The soy milk powders usually do not taste as good as packaged soy milk. These types of soy milk are not meant or suitable for infants. They do not contain enough protein, food energy or other nutrients for babies. Infant soy formula is available from all pharmacies.

Cashew Nut Milk

1 cup raw cashews
1 tsp. honey (optional)
2½ cups water

¼ tsp. vanilla extract
(Optional)

Blend the nuts to form a fine meal. Gradually add water to the blender to form a milky consistency. Use less water if you want cashew cream. Try using juice instead of water if you are avoiding sweeteners.

Sunflower Seed Milk

½ cup sunflower seeds
2 cups water
2 cups water

1 Tbs. honey or maple syrup
(optional)

Blend the seeds to form a fine meal. Gradually add water to the blender to form a milky consistency. Use less water if you want sunflower cream. Try using juice instead of water if you are avoiding sweeteners. Use the milk immediately before the sesame residue settles or strain it and use the seed powder in another recipe or on top of a cereal.

Dandelion Coffee/Espresso

1 tsp. ground, roasted   1 cup water
   dandelion root

Simmer or percolate for 10 minutes. Do not make too strong.

Chicory Coffee

1 Tsp. ground chicory root   2 cups water

Make as you would coffee with a filter or percolator.

DAY TWO

Grape Juice Sangria

1.5 litre grape juice   3 cups sparkling water
½ papaya, thinly sliced   12 ice cubes
10 strawberries or other
   berries, thinly sliced

In a pitcher, or a bowl for a party, mix the juice and fruit slices. Stir in the sparkling water and the ice cubes just before serving.

Sesame Milk

½ cup sesame seeds   1 Tbs. honey or maple syrup
2 cups water   (optional)

Blend the seeds to form a fine meal. Gradually add water to the blender to form a milky consistency. Use less water if you want sesame cream. Try using juice instead of water if you are avoiding sweeteners. Use the milk immediately before the sesame residue settles or strain it and use the seed powder in another recipe or on top of a cereal.

Atole

This pre-Columbian Mexican beverage is still regularly served. It is best when served hot off the stove. Great on cool, wet days, If you are sensitive to sugar, this is not for you.

3 cups water
1 stick cinnamon
2 Tbs. corn syrup

½ cup masa harina or corn flour
¼ cup water

Bring 3 cups of water and the cinnamon stick to a boil. Remove from heat and let stand for 1 hour. Remove cinnamon stick. Mix corn flour into ¼ cup water until smooth. Slowly add to cinnamon water. Stir in the corn syrup and stir over medium heat until the atole starts to thicken. If too thick, add more water. Makes 3 servings. It can be varied by flavouring with pureed fruits rather than cinnamon.

DAY THREE

Carrot and Celery Juice

Juice 1 stick of celery and 5-6 carrots. Delicious and filling.

Rice Cooler

2 cups white rice
½ cup hazelnuts
2 Tbs. cinnamon
8 cups hot water

½ cup date jam (page 188)
1 tsp. vanilla extract
ice cubes

Soak rice overnight in water with almonds and cinnamon. Then drain and save the liquid. Blend half the drained rice/almond mixture and add 1 cup of the saved liquid and ¼ cup of the date jam. Repeat with the rest of the rice/almond mixture. Strain the mixture through a fine sieve into a pitcher and stir in the vanilla extract. Refrigerate until cool and serve with ice. Great for a hot day.

Orange/Grapefruit Juice Punch

1.5 litre orange or grapefruit   *1 kiwi fruit, thinly sliced*
    juice   *3 cups sparkling water*
1 orange, thinly sliced   *12 ice cubes*

In a pitcher, or a bowl for a party, mix the juice and fruit slices. Blood orange or ruby grapefruit slices look very good. Stir in the sparkling water and the ice cubes just before serving.

Coconut Milk

1 cup hot water   *½ cup shredded coconut*

Combine the water and coconut in a blender. Blend for two minutes. Do not overfill the blender or the milk will fly out the top. Strain if you prefer a smooth milk. Leave the coconut in if you want more coconut flavour and texture in baked items. If no blender is available, pour boiling water over coconut. Let stand ½ hour and squeeze out with cheesecloth. Cool before use.

Hazelnut/Filbert Milk

1 cup raw hazelnuts   *2½ cups water*

Blend the nuts to form a fine meal. Gradually add water to the blender to form a milky consistency. Use less water if you want hazelnut cream. Try using juice instead of water if you are avoiding sweeteners. Use the milk immediately before the nut residue settles or strain it and use the nut powder in another recipe or on top of a cereal.
You could also use this recipe substituting pine nuts.

Lemon Tea

Squeeze 1 teaspoon of fresh lemon juice into a cup of hot water. Add a half teaspoon of honey if you like. Very soothing.

Apple Juice Cider

1.5 *litre apple juice*   1 *apple, thinly sliced*
1 *peach or plum thinly sliced*   3 *cups sparkling water*
    or 10 pitted cherries   12 *ice cubes*

In a pitcher, or a bowl for a party, mix the juice and fruit slices. Stir in the sparkling water and the ice cubes just before serving.

Apple Cider

3 *cups apple cider*   1 *cinnamon stick*
3 *cloves*

Gently simmer cider and spices. Do not allow to boil. Simmering pieces of apple, pear or peach will make this a special drink. Children will enjoy fishing out the pieces of fruit to eat them.

Almond Milk

1 *cup raw almonds*   2½ *cups water*

Blend the nuts to form a fine meal. Gradually add water to the blender to form a milky consistency. Use less water if you want almond cream. Try using juice instead of water if you are avoiding sweeteners. Use the milk immediately before the nut residue settles or strain it and use the nut powder in another recipe or on top of a cereal. Use this recipe substituting macadamia nuts or Brazil nuts too.

Hot Apricot

1¾ *cup apple-apricot juice*   2 *cinnamon sticks*
(combine your own)   ¼ *tsp. whole cloves*

Buy apricot juice or simmer sliced apricots slowly and blend. Strain the juice. Combine with cloves in small saucepan. Bring to boil then reduce heat and simmer 5 minutes. Strain into 2 mugs. Add a cinnamon stick to each. You can also substitute with apple-peach juice.

Grains

DAY ONE

Spelt & Kamut

If you tolerate these relatives of wheat (most people allergic to wheat do not tolerate them) they can be cooked like rice into a cereal. If you have a grain mill, crack the kernels and cook with two parts water into a cereal like bulgar.

DAY TWO

Millet

Millet is in the grass family but usually not cross-reactive with wheat. It has no gluten and so is suitable for people with celiac disease. It is a small round, cream coloured grain. Close relatives are bajra from India and teff from Ethiopia. Sorghum is a similar but different grain also called milo, Kaffir corn or raji. It has long been a staple grain in southern Africa. Prepare it just as you would millet. It is slightly chewier. Some natural food sores stock it. It is often available at feed stores, since in North America it is usually used for chicken feed. If you buy it at a feed store be sure that it has not been treated or sprayed with chemicals.

Millet can be cooked into porridge and eaten as it is or pureed after cooking and made into balls to add to soups and stews. To add flavour when cooking millet place it in a heavy saucepan and roast over medium heat until it is slightly browned then add water. Use 3½ parts water to 1 part millet. Use cooked millet in place of rice or cracked wheat in any recipe.

Millet Cereal

3½-4 cups water   *1 cup millet*

Wash millet thoroughly. Bring water to a boil, add millet (soak overnight to hasten cooking if desired), then simmer gently for 30 minutes. Sweeten with maple syrup and fresh fruit. Add a non-dairy milk if desired to increase flavour and protein count or add dry roasted nuts.

Teff

Teff is the staple grain of Ethiopia. It is a very small grain and nutty in flavour. It can be found in several colours, usual brown or ivory. To cook as a grain use three parts water to one part teff. Try it combined with millet or corn meal.

Cornmeal (Polenta)

½ cup cornmeal   *2 cups cold water*

Add cornmeal to water and bring to boil while stirring. Cook 15 minutes or longer. Lower heat and stir frequently until the cornmeal has thickened. If too thick add more water. You may want to add ¼ tsp. salt plus fruit or vanilla.

Flaxseed

This is really the seed of the flax or linen plant. Fresh seeds can be planted to grow a lovely pale blue flower on a foot high stem. Use it whole or broken to give texture to baking, broken as a source of fibre or soaked as an egg replacer (see below)

Flaxseed Egg Replacer

Boil 1 tablespoon flaxseed in 1 cup water for 15 minutes. Add to muffins etc as a binder.

DAY THREE

Amaranth and Quinoa

These two are seeds, not really grains at all, of weeds in the goosefoot family. They were originally used by the Incas in the Andes of South America. They will cook up into grain like cereals that can be used instead of rice or cracked wheat. They have mild flavours that are slightly different from each other. For instructions on cooking see below.

Hot Amaranth Cereal

1 cup amaranth   *2 cups water*

Combine in a saucepan. Cover and bring to a boil. Reduce heat and simmer for 25 minutes. Serve with fruit and nuts. Serves 3. For one serving use ¼ cup amaranth and 1 cup water. Use amaranth to replace millet in any recipe.

Quinoa Pilaff

1 cup quinoa   *2 cups water*

Rinse well under running water. Bring water to boil. When rapidly boiling add quinoa. Add herbs or spices such as cinnamon or oregano to complement the rest of the meal. Reduce heat and let simmer until all the water absorbed. Use quinoa to replace millet in any recipe. Serves 3 people.

Rice

There are many different forms of rice but all are cross-reactive. If you are allergic to rice avoid white, brown, parboiled, converted, red, black and glutinous or sweet rice. Wild rice is not related to ordinary rice and can be used if you are allergic to regular rice. Use it in pilaus, paella or any other rice recipe.

DAY FOUR

Oatmeal Porridge

2 cups water *1 cup oats*

Cook on low heat. Sweeten and serve with seed or nut milk.

Raw-soaked Oats

Soak 1 cup oats in 2-3 cups water overnight. Serve with peaches or apricots etc. Delicious!

Breads, Crackers and Flat Breads

DAY ONE

Herbed Chickpea Skillet Bread

1 cup chickpea flour
1½ tsp. baking powder
3 Tbs. oil
1 cup water

Any of: ⅓ cup minced
    scallion, 2 Tbs. parsley,
    1 tsp. fresh chopped basil,
    ½ tsp. rosemary or oregano

In a bowl combine the dry ingredients. Add liquid and herbs. Let stand for 15 minutes. In a heavy oven proof skillet with 7-8 inches bottom diameter, heat 2 Tbs. oil over moderate to high heat and add batter. Spread evenly. Drizzle remaining oil over it. Bake in pre-heated oven at 400° F. for 15 minutes. Invert a large plate over the skillet and invert the bread onto it. Slide it back into skillet and bake for 10 minutes more or until brown.

Spicy Pumpkin Bread

¾ cup chickpea flour
¾ cup tapioca flour (skip
    tapioca on next rotation)
¾ tsp. baking powder
¼ Tbs. cinnamon
¼ tsp. salt
¼ tsp. nutmeg
¼ tsp. cloves

¼ tsp. ginger
½ cup chopped figs
¼ cup butter or oil
¼ cup honey or sweetener
2 eggs or alternative
¾ tsp. vanilla
1 cup pumpkin (cooked or
    pureed)

Combine dry ingredients together and mix well. Combine wet ingredients together and mix well. Gradually and gently blend wet and dry ingredients together. Spread in a bread pan lined with brown paper and bake at 350° F. for about 1 hour until a knife inserted in the middle comes out clean.

Poppy Banana Bread

1¾ cup chickpea flour
2¼ tsp. baking powder
¼ cup fig spread (see
    page 187)
¼ cup poppy or sunflower
    seeds (optional)

1-1¼ cup banana pulp
¼ cup water
¼ cup oil
½ tsp. coriander

Combine the dry ingredients and add to the creamed wet ingredients. Bake in a 8½x4½ pan at 350°F. for about 40 minutes.

Chickpea Crackers

1½ cups chickpea flour
½ tsp. baking powder
¼ tsp. salt

1 Tbs. oil
1 cup water
¼ cup poppy seeds (optional)

Pre-heat oven to 325°. Combine chickpea flour, baking powder and salt. Stir in oil and water. Pour into 7x11 inch pan. Spread the batter on the pan to form an even layer. Sprinkle with poppy seeds if you like. Bake 20 minutes and then cut into squares with a sharp knife. Then bake for another 20 minutes.

DAY TWO

Corn Meal Crackers

1 cup corn meal
1 cup corn flour
¼ tsp. salt

1 tsp. baking powder
¼ tsp. oil
1½ cup water

Combine corn meal, corn flour, salt and baking powder. Add oil and water and stir till a thick dough is formed. Roll out on a cookie sheet as thin as possible, about ¼ inch. Cut into squares. Bake at 350° for 10 minutes.

Corn Only Corn Bread

⅛ cup corn syrup
1 cup milk alternative
5 Tbs. oil
1 egg or 2 Tbs. flaxseed egg
    replacer (see page 74)

1 cup corn meal
1 cup corn flour
3 tsp. baking powder
½ tsp. salt

Combine oil, corn syrup and liquid. Beat in egg. Mix dry ingredients and add to liquid mixture. Combine and bake at 350° F. for about 20 minutes. Best baked in a pie plate or a small loaf tin.

DAY THREE

Rice Crackers

Top with hazelnut butter, shrimp pate or goat's milk cheese.

Rice Wrappers

These thin flexible wrappers are available from Chinese or Vietnamese grocers. Wrap them around vegetables or stuff with your favourite sandwich filling. Use instead of wheat or corn tortillas. To prepare briefly dip the dry wrapper in cold water and handle carefully.

Rice Crackers

11½ cups rice flour
½ tsp. baking powder
¼ tsp. salt

1 Tbs. oil
1 cup water

Pre-heat oven to 325°. Combine chickpea flour, baking powder and salt. Stir in oil and water. Pour into 7x11 inch pan. Spread the batter on the pan to form an even layer. Bake 20 minutes and then cut into squares with a sharp knife. Then bake for another 20 minutes.

Mochi

This is a chewy rice product with a crisp crust. It is made from cooked and crushed glutinous rice. It is often available frozen, or fresh from Japanese stores. Bake it in an oven at 350° until it puffs up and a crust has formed. It can be cut open and a filling or topping added or eaten as it is.

Tortillas

1 cup Masa harina	*½ cup warm water*

Work water into the masa to make a soft dough. Shape into a ball, cover and let sit for 20 minutes. Divide into 6 balls. Line a tortilla press with plastic and press each or use a heavy skillet to make a thin flat tortilla. If necessary, add a little masa or water if too sticky or crumbly. Cook on a preheated skillet until lightly spotted with brown. Turn once. Alternatively, you can buy frozen tortillas and lightly bake or fry them.

Carrot Bread

1 cup rice flour	*¼ tsp. cloves*
½ cup tapioca flour or 1¼ cup amaranth flour instead of rice and tapioca	*1 tsp. ginger*
	½ cup date jam
	¼ cup oil
2 tsp. baking soda	*1 cup nut milk or carrot or orange juice*
¼ tsp. cinnamon	
¼ tsp. salt	*¾ cup grated carrots*
¼ tsp. nutmeg	*¾ tsp. vanilla*

Combine dry ingredients together and mix well. Combine wet ingredients together and mix well. Gradually and gently blend wet and dry ingredients together. Batter will be very thick. Pour into loaf pan lined with brown paper and bake at 350°F. for about 1 hour until a knife inserted in the middle comes out clean.

DAY FOUR

Oat Crackers

1½ cups oat flour
1 Tbs. oil
pinch baking powder

1 cup water
pinch salt

Pre-heat oven to 325°F. Pour into 7x11 pan. Spread to even layer. Bake 20 minutes and then cut into squares. Bake for another 20 minutes.

Experiment to find your favourite type of cracker by using light buckwheat flour, chickpea flour or others. They can be topped with poppy or sesame seeds.

Buckwheat or Oat Crackers

1½ cups buckwheat or oat
  flour
½ tsp. baking powder
¼ tsp. salt

1 Tbs. oil
1 cup water

Pre-heat oven to 325°. Combine flour, baking powder and salt. Stir in oil and water. Pour into 7x11 inch pan. Spread the batter on the pan to form an even layer. Bake 20 minutes and then cut into squares with a sharp knife. Then bake for another 20 minutes.

Oat Biscuits

1 cup oat flour, sifted
2½ tsp. baking powder
1½ Tbs. oil

¼ cup water or juice
¼ tsp. salt
1 Tbs. maple syrup

Mix dry ingredients. Stir oil and maple syrup together and stir into flour mixture until crumbly. Add water to make a soft dough. Form dough into small biscuits and place on a greased cookie sheet. Bake at 425°F. for 15-20 minutes. Makes 8 biscuits.

Buckwheat Currant Bread

1 cup currants	½ cup chopped almonds
1⅔ cups water or juice	1 cup arrowroot
½ cup oil	1 tsp. baking soda
½ tsp. vitamin C powder	2 tsp. cinnamon
1 cup light buckwheat flour	¼ tsp. cloves

Simmer currants and water together for 10 minutes. Then add oil and vitamin C powder. Mix together the dry ingredients and add to the liquid. Pour into an 8 inch square pan and bake at 400° F. for 20 minutes. Eat while warm. If you dislike the strong flavour of dark buckwheat flour, make your own light buckwheat flour. Grind unroasted buckwheat groats in a blender for a couple of minutes, ½ cup at a time. Sieve the flour and regrind the large pieces with more groats until you have enough.

NON-ROTATING

Yuca/Cassava Pancakes with Chives or Parsley

1 lb. fresh yuca or cassava, peeled or frozen and thawed	6 Tbs. oil
2 Tbs. chopped fresh chives or parsley	½ cup fresh ground hazelnuts (make in blender)
salt and pepper to taste	1 egg beaten

Boil cassava until easily pierced with fork-about 35 minutes. Drain well. Puree in processor. Press through coarse sieve into bowl. Stir in chives, then egg. Season generously with salt and pepper. Form patties, 3 inches across, ½ inch thick. Coat completely with hazelnuts and shake off excess. Heat oil in preheated heavy medium skillet over medium high heat. Add patties and cook on both sides until golden brown-about 5 minutes. Remove using slotted spatula and drain on towels. Serve hot. Makes four servings.

Corn-Oat Skillet Bread

¾ cup rolled oats	1 cup liquid (water, soy milk)
¼ cup yellow corn meal	⅓ cup minced scallion
1½ tsp. baking powder	2 Tbs. minced parsley leaves
½ tsp. baking soda	3 Tbs. oil pinch of cayenne

In a bowl, combine the dry ingredients. Add the wet ingredients and let stand ten minutes. In a heavy oven proof skillet 7-8 inches across the bottom heat 2 Tbs. of oil on moderate high element till hot, add batter, spread it evenly and drizzle remaining oil over it. Bake the bread in the middle of the hot oven for 15 minutes. Invert a large plate over the skillet and invert the bread onto it. Slide the bread back into the skillet bake again for 10 minutes or until underside is brown. Let bread cool for 5 minutes. Cut into wedges to serve. You can use combinations of other flours e.g. chickpea and oat.

Banana Bread #1 - Rice, Soy Flour

1 cup rice flour	2 ripe bananas
½ cup soy flour	¼ cup oil
2 Tbs. tapioca flour	¼ cup sweetener
2 tsp. baking powder	¼ tsp. salt
2 eggs	

Mix rice, soy and tapioca flours with baking soda and salt. Blend bananas, oil, sweetener and eggs. Mix into dry ingredients. Bake at 350° F. for 45 minutes in 4x8 inch bread pan.

Banana Bread #2 - Amaranth Flour

Mix 1 cup amaranth flour and ½ cup tapioca flour and 2 tsp. baking powder. Proceed as for banana bread #1 substituting these flours.

Gingerbread

1¼ cup rice flour
1½ cup corn starch
1 tsp. baking soda
1 tsp. cinnamon
¼ tsp. clove

¼ tsp. ginger
⅓ cup molasses or sweetener
½ cup oil
1 cup boiling water
2 eggs-well beaten

Mix dry ingredients. Add molasses, oil and then water. Add eggs. Bake at 325° F. for 45 minutes in 9x9 inch pan. If you like, add ⅓ cup raisins or chopped nuts.

Hotcakes

1 cup soya flour
1 Tbs. oil
4 to 6 oz. water

pinch baking powder
1 cup corn flour
pinch salt

Mix dry ingredients, add oil and water and blend. Use 1 tsp. oil to cook ¼ of the batter at a time in a small griddle.

Quick Bread

⅔ cup rice flour
⅓ cup potato flour
½ cup oat bran
½ cup chopped raisins or
   other dried fruit
½ tsp. cinnamon

1 tsp. vanilla
2 tsp. baking soda
1 cup nut or soy milk
1 egg or replacer for binding
1 mashed banana or ½ cup
   apricots or pumpkin

Combine flours, oat bran, raisins, cinnamon and baking soda. Combine nut milk, egg, oil, banana and vanilla. Then mix contents of both bowls together. Pour one cup of batter into each of three well-oiled soup cans. Cover with foil and steam them on a rack in a large covered pot for one hour. Let loaves cool before slicing. The loaves will keep for about one week if wrapped in plastic and refrigerated.

Breakfast

Wondering what to have for breakfast? See the sections on Grains, Breads, Crackers and Flat Breads, Breakfast, Pancakes, Waffles, Muffins, Vegetables, Fruit, Fish, Meat and Fowl, Puddings, Fruit Sauces, Jams and Spreads.

DAY ONE

Scrambled Tofu

Cut firm tofu into small pieces. Tofu can then be scrambled like egg (in an oiled skillet). Cook well. Add seasonings such as saffron, basil, curry.

Tofu Yogurt

Blend a cube of soft tofu into a smooth consistency. Mix with ½ tsp. vanilla, 2 Tbs. honey (optional) and ¼ tsp. ascorbic acid. Add fruit and mix gently.

Chickpea Biscuits

1 cup chickpea flour
2 tsp. baking powder
½ Tbs. oil
1 Tbs. poppy seeds (optional)

¼ tsp. salt
1 Tbs. honey (optional)
¼ cup water or soy milk or
  juice

Mix dry ingredients. Stir oil and honey together and add to flour mixture. Add water to make a soft dough. Form dough into small balls and place on an oiled cookie sheet. Bake at 375° F. for 15-20 minutes. Best when warm. These can be very heavy. Some people do not like the taste of chickpea flour.

Fruit and Nuts

Slice a banana or use pieces of pineapple or melon and serve with nut or seed milk. Sweeten with honey if desired.

Peanut Butter and Banana

Slice banana lengthwise and spread with peanut butter. Great!!

See recipes for: Tuna Salad, Mackerel, Oat Crepe, Buckwheat Crepe,

DAY TWO

Morning Millet Casserole

1 cup washed millet	cinnamon
3½ cups water or soy milk	sweetener or chopped fruit
2 Tbs. oil	

Bring water or soy milk to a boil. Add washed millet and a dash of salt and simmer for 35-45 minutes. Add oil and cool. Then spread mixture on cookie sheet and sprinkle with sweetener or chopped fruit and cinnamon. Bake for 20 minutes in a hot oven. Serve with apple sauce or stewed fruit.

See recipes for: Millet Cereal, Millet Raisin Pudding, Cornmeal (Polenta), Indian Pudding, Tortillas, Tacos, Cod or Carp, Fruit and Nuts

DAY THREE

See recipes for: Brown Rice Pudding, Rice Cakes, Citrus Fruit Salad, Red Snapper, Date Jam, Date Nut Jam, Non-Dairy Tapioca Pudding, Fruit Juice Tapioca Pudding, Rice Filbert Muffins, Carrot Bread, Amaranth Cereal, Herring, Sardine, Quinoa Cereal,

DAY FOUR

Oat Breakfast Bars

½ cup + 2 Tbs. warm water   1 cup currants
1½ cups oat flour   ¾ cup quick rolled oats
2 Tbs. almonds or other nuts   ½ tsp. salt
  (finely chopped)

Blend water, nuts and currants together. Combine dry ingredients. Add liquid mixture to dry. Knead into stiff dough. Place on cookie sheet. Spread with hands to ¼-½ inches thick. Bake at 325° F. for 45 minutes.

See recipes for: Oatmeal Porridge, Raw-soaked Oats, Plum and Pear Salad, Applesauce, Prune Spread, Oat Biscuits, Sweet Potato Muffins

NON-ROTATING RECIPES

Zucchini Bread

3 cups grated zucchini   1½ cups rice flour
2 eggs   1 tsp. pumpkin spice
½ cup brown sugar or honey   ½ tsp. baking soda
  (optional)   ½ tsp. baking powder
3 tsp. vanilla   1 cup chopped walnuts
1½ cups soy flour   3 Tbs. oil

Beat eggs, blend in sugar and add zucchini, oil and vanilla. Combine dry ingredients and add to wet ingredients. Pour into 2 small loaf tins or an 8x10 inch pan. Bake at 325° F. for 45 minutes.

Pancakes

If the pancake centre is undercooked then the pan is too hot.
If the pancakes are hard then either the pan is too hot or the batter
was too dry or there was not enough oil in the recipe.
If the pancake is not browning then the pan is too cool or there is
no sweetener in the recipe. It will not brown well without
sweetener.

DAY ONE

Peanut Tofu Pancakes

¼ cup roasted peanuts without
 skins
¼ cup soft tofu
2 Tbs. chickpea flour

2 Tbs. water
1 Tbs. oil
½ tsp. baking powder

In a blender puree the peanuts until they form a coarse flour. If you
cannot find roasted peanuts, roast unroasted peanuts carefully in a
heavy skillet over medium heat. Add the tofu, chickpea flour, water,
oil and baking powder to the blender and puree until smooth. If too
thick add a little more water. Batter should flow slightly when
poured. Fry each side on a well oiled skillet until golden. Serve with
fruit or as a side dish with a soup or stew.

Spelt Pancakes

1 cup spelt flour
2 tsp. baking powder

2 Tbs. oil
½ cup soy milk or water

Mix flour and baking powder. Add oil and soy milk. Stir quickly
leaving any lumps that form. If too thick add a little more water.
Batter should flow slightly when poured. Fry each side on a well oiled
pan until golden.

DAY TWO

Teff Pancakes

1 cup teff flour   ¼ tsp. salt
1½ tsp. baking powder   1 Tbs. oil
1½ tsp. arrowroot or tapioca   1 cup fruit juice
   flour (skip in next rotation)

Mix teff flour, baking powder, arrowroot or tapioca flour and salt. Add oil and fruit juice. Let sit for a few minutes until it thickens slightly. Fry each side on a well oiled pan. The pancakes will tend to stick slightly to the pan.

Millet Latkes

2 cups cooked millet   ⅓ cup raisin jam
2 eggs   (see page 187)
½ tsp. cinnamon (optional)

Beat millet and eggs together until free of lumps. Add raisins and cinnamon if used. Form into thin pancakes and saute in a well oiled pan over medium heat until browned on each side. Serve with fruit.

Potato Latkes

3 large potatoes   1 large onion (optional)
1 egg   salt and pepper to taste
¼ cup corn or millet flour   ½ tsp. basil (optional)

Grate potatoes finely or run through a food processor. Squeeze out as much of the liquid as possible. Grate onion finely. Add to potatoes and mix with eggs and flour. Add salt, pepper and basil. Add oil to hot skillet. Ladle spoonfuls of batter onto the hot skillet forming into pancakes. Fry quickly until brown and turn. Drain on paper.

Chickpea Crepe

1 cup chickpea flour
½ cup water or more if needed

¼ tsp. salt
¼ cup tofu (optional)

Blend until smooth. Pour on hot, well oiled griddle. Cook 2 minutes then flip. Cook 30 seconds or until golden. Stuff with fresh fruit for breakfast e.g. bananas or pineapple or cooked beans, beef, fish, etc. for lunch or dinner.

If not rotating, use a 50% mixture of chickpea and buckwheat flours.

DAY THREE

Rice Pancakes

⅞ cup brown rice flour
2 Tbs. rice bran
1 tsp. baking powder
¼ tsp. salt

¾ cup water, nut milk or juice
1 Tbs. oil
¼ cup blueberries (optional)

Mix together rice flour and bran, baking powder and salt. Add blueberries if desired. Add oil and water to flour. Batter should not be too thick. If necessary add more water. Heat a skillet and oil well when the skillet is hot. Pour 3 inch pancakes and watch carefully since the pancakes tend to stick and burn easily. Cook until lightly golden and then turn. Serve with date jam or fruit.

Fluffy Rice Pancakes

1¼ cup brown rice flour
½ cup tapioca flour
¼ cup sweet rice flour
1 tsp. baking powder

2 cups water or nut milk or juice
2 Tbs. oil

Sift together dry ingredients. Add blueberries if desired. Mix liquid ingredients and add to dry. Cook until lightly golden.

Hazelnut Crepe

1 cup hazelnut flour
½ cup tapioca flour
2 tsp. baking powder
1 cup water or orange juice

1½ Tbs. oil
2 Tbs. date jam (see page 188 optional)

Make hazelnut flour by chopping nuts in a blender until they are in a grainy powder form. Add tapioca flour, baking powder, water or orange juice, oil and date jam. Blend until smooth. Pour into a well-oiled, preheated skillet over medium heat, to thinly cover bottom. Cook 2 minutes or until top starts to dry. Turn and cook 30 seconds. Crepes are chewy, not fluffy. If not rotating, 2 Tbs. soft tofu can be added for lightness. Fill with blueberries, kiwi fruit, fish or meat.

Hazelnut Pancake

1 cup hazelnut flour
½ cup tapioca flour
2 tsp. baking powder
1 cup water or orange juice

1½ Tbs. oil
2 Tbs. date jam (see page 188 optional)

Make hazelnut flour by chopping nuts in a blender until they are in a grainy powder form. Add tapioca flour, baking powder, water or orange juice, oil and date jam. Spoon onto a well oiled skillet and cook each side until lightly browned. Serve with blueberries or kiwi fruit slices.

Tapioca Pancake

1 cup hazelnut flour (make in blender from whole nuts)
½ cup tapioca flour
2 tsp. baking powder

1 cup water or juice
1½ Tbs. oil
2 Tbs. rice syrup or date sugar (optional)

In a blender mix all ingredients well. Pour into a hot, oiled skillet and cook until done.

Tapioca Crepe

1 cup hazelnut flour (make in
   blender from whole nuts)
½ cup tapioca flour
2 tsp. baking powder

1 cup water or juice
1½ Tbs. oil
2 Tbs. rice syrup or date sugar
   (optional)

In a blender mix all ingredients well. Pour into a well-oiled, preheated skillet over medium heat, to thinly cover bottom. Cook 2 minutes or until top starts to dry. Turn and cook 30 seconds. Crepes are chewy, not fluffy. If not rotating, 2 Tbs. soft tofu can be added for lightness.

DAY FOUR

If you dislike the strong flavour of dark buckwheat flour, make your own light buckwheat flour. Grind unroasted buckwheat groats in a blender for a couple of minutes, ½ cup at a time. Sieve the flour and regrind the large pieces with more groats until you have enough.

Buckwheat Arrowroot Pancakes

1½ cups light buckwheat flour
½ cup arrowroot
1½ tsp. baking soda
water as needed

3 Tbs. oil
1 egg or replacer for leavening
   (optional)

Mix dry with dry, wet with wet. Blend together. Add more water to make crepes. Pour onto a hot skillet and cook until done.

Buckwheat Pancakes

1 cup light buckwheat flour
1 tsp. baking powder
1 cup oat flour
2 cups water

2 Tbs. oil
1 egg, well beaten or substitute
   for leavening (optional)

Mix dry with dry, wet with wet. Stir a little. Cook on hot skillet. Top with fruit and sweetener, e.g. maple syrup.

Buckwheat-Nut Pancakes

1⅓ cup buckwheat flour	¼ tsp. salt
l cup almond or Brazil nut meal	1½ cup water or almond milk
1 tsp. baking powder	2 Tbs. oil

Make nut meal by grinding nuts in a blender or coffee grinder. Combine buckwheat flour, nut meal, baking powder and salt and stir until lumps are broken up. Stir in the water or almond milk and the oil. Preheat skillet on a medium temperature stove. Pour small amounts of the batter into oiled and heated skillet to make 2 inch rounds. Allow to cook slowly and turn when the bottom is browned and brown the other side.

Oat-Nut Pancakes

1⅓ cup oat flour	¼ tsp. salt
l cup almond or Brazil nut meal	1½ cup water or almond milk
1 tsp. baking powder	2 Tbs. oil

Make nut meal by grinding nuts in a blender or coffee grinder. Combine oat flour, nut meal, baking powder and salt and stir until lumps are broken up. Stir in the water or almond milk and the oil. Preheat skillet on a medium temperature stove. Pour small amounts of the batter into oiled and heated skillet to make 2 inch rounds. Allow to cook slowly and turn when the bottom is browned and brown the other side.

Arrowroot Pancakes

1 cup nut or seed flour	1 cup water or juice
½ cup arrowroot powder	1½ Tbs. oil
2 tsp. baking powder	2 Tbs. maple syrup (optional)

In a blender mix all ingredients well. Pour onto a hot, oiled skillet and cook until done.

Oat Crepe

1 cup oat flour   1 cup apple juice or water
½ cup arrowroot flour   1½ Tbs. oil
2 tsp. baking powder

Pre-heat skillet to medium heat and then lightly oil pan. Blend all the above ingredients. Pour into skillet to produce a thin even crepe. Cook 2 minutes or until top starts to dry. Flip and cook 30 seconds. Roll up with warm fruit and/or nuts for breakfast or with fish, meat or vegetable for dinner.

Buckwheat Crepe

1 cup light buckwheat flour   2 cups apple juice or water
½ cup arrowroot flour   1½ Tbs. oil
2 tsp. baking powder

Pre-heat skillet to medium heat and then lightly oil pan. Blend all the ingredients. More liquid may be needed to make a thin smooth batter. Pour into skillet to produce a thin even crepe. Cook 2 minutes or until top starts to dry. Flip and cool for 30 seconds. Roll up with warm fruit for breakfast.

NON-ROTATING RECIPES

Oat Pancakes

3 cups rolled oats   ¾ cup oat, barley or tapioca
3 eggs beaten or substitute for   flour
   binding   1 Tbs. sweetener

Soak rolled oats in 1 pint water for 3 hours. Add eggs, sweetener and flour. Drop small pancakes in frying pan with heated oil and fry until crisp on both sides.

Jicama Pancakes

3 cups jicama
juice of one lemon
1 Tbs. chive or other
  herbs
1 egg

1 Tbs. tapioca or arrowroot
  flour
¼ tsp. salt
2 tsp. chile powder (optional)

Peel the jicama and shred with a coarse grater. Pour the lemon juice over the jicama and drain in a colander for 15 minutes. Squeeze out the remaining moisture. Blot with paper towels. Beat the egg and mix al the ingredients. Fry quickly on each side until crisp and brown.

Oat and Apple Pancakes

1½ cups rolled oats
1½ tsp. ground almonds
pinch of salt
1 lb. grated apples

1 cup water, nut or soy milk
2 egg yolks
2 stiffly beaten egg whites

Mix oats with water and let stand for one hour. Add the egg yolks and fold in the whites, almonds and salt. Fold the apples into the batter. Spoon batter into a little hot oil in a frying pan. Serve with maple syrup and cinnamon.

Almond Tofu Pancakes

Use the recipe for Peanut Tofu Pancakes and substitute almonds for peanuts. You could substitute any nut or seed for the peanuts.

Blueberry Pancakes

1 cup blueberries-fresh or
frozen
2 cups liquid-soy milk, juice,
water
1 tsp. baking soda
1 tsp. baking powder

2 Tbs. oil
2 cups flour, e.g.1 cup
buckwheat, ½ cup soy,
½ cup rice
2 tsp. flax seed
½ cup water

Simmer flax seed in ½ cup water for 10 minutes and then cool. Sift dry ingredients together. Combine wet ingredients and then add wet to dry ingredients. Add blueberries and cook.

Rice Pancakes

2 cups rice flour
½ tsp. baking soda
1 egg or ½ cup tofu
1 tsp. baking powder
¼ cup oil

1½ cups soy milk or other milk
substitute with 2 tsp. vinegar or
lemon juice)
1 Tbs. honey
¼ tsp. salt

Combine everything except the rice flour until smooth. Add rice flour and blend until smooth. Cook in lightly oiled pan. Make small 4 inch pancakes.

Waffles

All of these waffles will be more enjoyable if ample fruit and allowed sweeteners are used on top. They will be heavier than wheat waffles. Be careful about cooking times. They require close watching to not over cook. If they are too dry or hard, check if they were cooked too long or at too high a temperature. If the waffles stick check to see if the waffle iron was oiled enough or if the temperature is too high.

DAY ONE

Chickpea Waffle

1¼ cups chickpea flour   1½ Tbs. oil
1 tsp. baking powder   ¾ cup water
¼ cup soft tofu (optional)

Mix the chickpea flour and baking powder. Blend together the tofu, oil and water. Stir into the flour and let sit for a couple of minutes. Pour half of the mixture into the heated waffle iron and cook till done. Makes two double waffles.

Spelt Waffles

1 cup spelt flour   2 Tbs. oil
2 tsp. baking powder   ¾ cup soy milk or water

Mix flour and baking powder. Add oil and soy milk. Stir quickly, without over beating. Pour half of the mixture into the heated waffle iron and cook till done. Makes two double waffles.

DAY TWO

Corn Waffle

1¼ cups corn flour   1½ Tbs. oil
1 tsp. baking powder   1 cup water or sesame milk
1 egg

Mix the corn flour and baking powder. Blend together the egg, oil and water. Stir into the flour and let sit for a couple of minutes. Pour half of the mixture into the heated waffle iron and cook till done. Makes two double waffles. Corn flour tends to produce drier products than wheat.

DAY THREE

Rice Waffle

1 cup brown rice flour
1 Tbs. sweet rice flour
1 tsp. baking powder
1 Tbs. oil

¼ cup date jam (see page 188)
1 ⅞ cups water

Mix flours and baking powder. Blend together oil, date jam and most of the water. Add to flour mixture. Add rest of water to make slightly thick batter. It will thicken as it stands. Pour half into pre-heated and well oiled waffle iron. Do not make the waffle too thick or it will not cook completely. Makes two double waffles.

DAY FOUR

Oat Waffle

1¼ cups oat flour
¼ cup prune spread (see page 189)

1 tsp. baking powder
1½ Tbs. oil
¾ cup water

Mix the oat flour and baking powder. Blend together the prune spread, oil and water. Stir into the flour and let sit for a couple of minutes. Pour half of the mixture into the heated waffle iron and cook till done. Makes two double waffles. If not rotating add ¼ cup soft tofu to the water and oil to make a lighter waffle.

Muffins

If the muffins are undercooked then the batter is too moist or the baking time is too short or the oven is not hot enough.

If the muffins are too crumbly then add more moisteners eg. oil or grated/mashed vegetables or fruit.

DAY ONE

Barley Muffins

2 cups barley flour (if
    tolerated)
½ tsp. salt
2 cups milk (peanut, cashew
    or soy) or water or juice

¼ cup oil
2 tsp. baking powder
½ cup honey or carob syrup
    (optional)
¼ tsp. vanilla

Mix wet ingredients with wet, dry ingredients with dry. Add wet to dry mixture and stir lightly until slightly lumpy. Add presoaked pieces of figs or pineapple chunks if desired. Serve with peanut or cashew butter. Bake at 350° F. for 20 minutes.

Pineapple Chickpea Muffins

1 Tbs. psyllium husk powder
1 cup pineapple juice or water
½ cup mashed banana or fig
    spread (see page 187)

3 Tbs. oil
2 cups chickpea flour
2 tsp. baking powder
¼ cup poppy seeds (optional)

Combine psyllium with 3 Tbs. water and then add pineapple juice, banana or fig spread and oil. Mix flour, baking powder and poppy seeds and add to juice mixture. Bake at 350° F. for 20 minutes. Makes 9 muffins. If you like add unsweetened carob chips for a chocolate flavour.

Spelt Muffins

4 dried figs
1 cup spelt flour
2 Tsp. baking powder

2 Tbs. oil
¼ cup soy milk or water

Soak figs in water overnight or simmer until soft. in blender liquify with oil and soy milk until soft. Combine spelt flour and baking powder. Add fig mixture and mix with a minimum of stirring. If too thick add some of the fig soaking water. Bake at 400° for about 20 minutes. Makes six muffins.

Chickpea Muffins

2 cups chickpea flour
3 tsp. baking powder
1 Tbs. psyllium husk mixed
    with 3 Tbs. water

¾ cup water or juice
¼ cup poppy seeds (optional)
¼ cup honey (optional)
3 Tbs. oil

Combine dry ingredients and add to wet. Bake at 350° F. for 20 minutes. Makes 10 muffins. These can be very heavy. Some people do not like the taste of chick pea flour.

DAY TWO

Corn Muffins

1 cup sesame milk
6 Tbs. oil
⅓ cup raisin puree
½ tsp. salt
1 cup corn meal

3 eggs or 6 Tbs. flaxseed egg
    replacer (see page 74)
1 cup corn flour
3 tsp. baking powder

Combine oil, raisin puree, sesame milk, and egg or egg replacer in blender. Mix corn meal, corn flour and baking powder and add to liquid mixture. Pour into oiled muffins tins. Combine well and bake at 350°. for about 20 minutes. Makes 10 muffins.

Blueberry Rice Muffins

¾ cup brown rice flour
1¼ rice bran
1 tsp. tapioca starch
1 tsp. baking powder
½ tsp. cinnamon

¾ cup blueberries
⅓ cup oil
¼ cup date jam (see
   page 188)
1 cup hazelnut milk or water

Combine rice flour, rice bran, tapioca starch baking powder, cinnamon and blueberries. Blend oil and date jam together and add to flour. Stir in milk or water. Pour into oiled muffin tins. Bake at 375° for 25 minutes. Makes 8 muffins.

Amaranth Muffins

1¾ cups amaranth flour or
   1¼ cups amaranth and
   ½ cup filbert flour
   (make in blender)
¼ cup tapioca flour
1 tsp. baking powder

1 tsp. cinnamon
½ tsp. vanilla (optional)
¼ cup oil
¾ cup water or juice
2-4 Tbs. date sugar or date
   jam (see page 188 optional)

Combine dry ingredients. Mix liquid ingredients and add to dry. Bake at 375° F. for 20 minutes. If you like, add 1 cup chopped dates or 1 cup blueberries or cranberries and/or ¼ cup chopped filberts to batter. Makes 8-10.

Rice Filbert Muffins

¾ cup rice
¼ cup sweet rice flour
2 Tbs. rice syrup or date sugar
   (optional)
¾ cup water or juice
3 tsp. ground filberts

1 Tbs. oil
2 tsp. baking powder
1 cup frozen or fresh
   blueberries or chopped
   dates (optional)

Mix oil, water and rice syrup together. Add to dry ingredients. Bake at 400° F. for 20 minutes. Makes 6.

Quinoa Orange Muffins

1¾ cups quinoa flour
¼ cup tapioca flour
1 tsp. baking powder
1 tsp. cinnamon
½ tsp. vanilla (optional)

¼ cup oil
¾ cup orange juice
1 tsp. grated rind of orange
2-4 Tbs. date sugar or date
    jam (see page 188 - optional)

Combine the flours, baking powder and cinnamon. Mix liquid
ingredients and finely grated orange. Add to dry ingredients. Bake
at 375° F. for 20 minutes. If you like, add 1 cup chopped dates or
¼ cup chopped walnuts to the batter. Makes 8-10.

DAY FOUR

Apple Oat Muffins

1¼ cup quick rolled oats
½ cup oat or light buckwheat
    flour (see page 62)
½ tsp. salt
1 tsp. baking powder

½ cup chopped prunes
1 cup coarsely grated apple
¼ cup oil
½ cup apple juice

Mix rolled oats, flour, salt, baking powder, prunes and grated apple.
Stir in oil and then juice until well combined. Pour into muffin tins
and bake at 375° for 20 minutes. Makes 10 muffins.

Fruit Muffins

1½ cups pear or apple juice
2 Tbs. arrowroot flour
2 Tbs. oil
1½ cups oat flour or light
    buckwheat flour
2 tsp. baking powder

½ tsp. cinnamon
¼ cup prune spread (see
    page 189)
1 cup chopped almonds
    (optional)

Mix fruit juice, prune spread and oil together. Add the arrowroot
flour, oat flour, cinnamon, almonds and baking powder and mix well.
Oil a muffin tin. Bake at 350°. for 20 minutes. Allow to cool.

Apricot Muffins

2 cup oat or buckwheat flour
2 tsp. baking powder
¼ cup oil
½ cup pitted prunes

1½ cup apricot puree (see
    page 188)
¼ cup chopped prunes
    (optional)

Mix flour and baking powder. Add prunes, oil and apricot puree to blender and blend until smooth. Add prunes if desired. Spoon batter into well oiled muffin tins. Bake at 350° for 20 minutes. Makes 10. Makes a heavy muffin. If not rotating add one egg to recipe.

Buckwheat/Arrowroot Muffins

1½ cup light buckwheat flour
    (see above)
½ cup arrowroot flour
2 tsp. baking powder

½-¾ water or juice
¼ cup oil
¼ cup maple syrup (optional)

Combine flours and baking powder. Add oil, honey and water and mix with a minimum of stirring. Bake at 400° F. for 20 minutes. Makes 9.

Sweet Potato Muffins

1 cup mashed sweet potato
¾ cup hot water
½ cup chopped nuts or seeds
2 Tbs. maple syrup

1 cup rolled oats
2 tsp. baking powder
2-3 Tbs. oil

Pour hot water over oats and let soak for a few minutes. Mix the rest of the ingredients together. Place in well greased muffin tins. Bake at 400° F. for 20 minutes. Makes 18 muffins.

Oat Bran Muffins #1

1¼ cup oat bran
1 cup oat flour
1 tsp. baking powder
¼ cup diced dried apples
 (optional)
¼ cup chopped almond
 (optional)

¼ cup grated apple (optional)
⅓ cup prune spread
2 Tbs. oil
1 tsp. almond extract
 (optional)
1 cup water or almond milk

Combine oat bran, oat flour, baking powder, dried apple, chopped almonds and grated apple. Blend together prune spread, oil, almond extract and water or almond milk and add to flour. Pour into oiled muffin tins. Bake at 425° for about 15 minutes. Makes 8 muffins.

NON-ROTATING

Oat Bran Muffins #2

2¼ cups oat bran cereal
¼ cup raisins or other dried
 fruit
1 Tbs. baking powder
¾ cup milk or alternative
¼ cup honey or maple syrup

2 beaten eggs or egg replacer
 for binding
¼ cup chopped nuts(optional)
¼ tsp. salt
2 Tbs. vegetable oil

Heat oven to 425° F. Grease bottom only of 12 medium sized muffin cups. Combine dry ingredients. Add milk, eggs, honey and oil. Mix until dry ingredients are moistened. Fill muffin tins ¾ full. Bake 15-17 minutes.

Apple Muffins

1-1½ cups pear or apple juice
¼ cup honey
1 egg or substitute for binding
2 Tbs. oil
1½ cups oat flour or rice flour

2 tsp. baking powder
½ tsp. cinnamon
1 cup chopped almonds
   (optional)

Mix fruit, honey, oil and eggs together. Add the other ingredients and mix well. Oil and flour a muffin tin. Bake at 350° F. for 20 minutes. Allow to cool.

Brown Rice Muffins

2 cups brown rice flour
2 tsp. baking powder
¾ cup milk alternative

1 Tbs. oil
4 Tbs. corn syrup or honey
1 egg or substitute for binding

Sift all dry ingredients together. Add milk, molasses and oil. Beat egg and add to mixture. Mix until smooth. Pour into oiled muffin pan. Fill ¾ full. Bake at 375° F. for 20-25 minutes. For variety add ¾ cup sunflower seeds, ¼ cup sesame seeds, ¼ cup chopped nuts or ⅓ cup raisins to dry ingredients. Makes 6.

Soy Muffins

1½ cups soy flour
2 tsp. baking powder
¼ tsp. salt
2 egg yolks
3 Tbs. sweetener

1 Tbs. soy oil
l cup soy or nut milk
¼ cup raisins
¼ cup chopped nuts (optional)
2 egg whites (beaten)

Mix together the soy flour, baking powder and salt. Cream the egg yolks with the sweetener and oil. Slowly add milk and pour into dry ingredients. Add nuts and raisins. Fold in stiff egg whites. pour into oiled muffin tins and bake at 375° F. for 30 minutes. Very heavy.

Soups

DAY ONE

Pumpkin Soup

3 cups pumpkin or squash   ⅛ tsp. nutmeg
3 cup soy or cashew milk   salt and pepper to taste
¼ tsp. cinnamon

Steam pumpkin or squash until it is soft. Peel it and combine in a blender with all of the other ingredients. Blend until it is smooth. Heat slowly, stirring to prevent burning until it is about to boil.

DAY TWO

Tomato Soup

2 cups fresh tomato   ½ tsp. basil
1 small onion, chopped   2 cups sesame milk
1 small garlic clove, minced   1 tsp. salt

Saute tomatoes, onion and garlic for 15 minutes. Add basil and continue to saute for two minutes. Add vegetables to blender with sesame milk and salt. Blend until smooth. Return to a pot and warm but do not boil.

Sesame Cream of Tomato Soup

2 cups fresh tomato puree   2 cups rich sesame milk
1 small onion, chopped   1 small garlic clove, minced
½ tsp. basil   1 tsp. salt
1 tsp. honey

Add onion, garlic and seasonings to tomato puree. In a blender, blend until smooth. Add sesame milk to blend. Warm but do not boil.

DAY THREE

Borscht

1 large carrot
3 large beets
1 celery stalk
2 bay leaves

2 Tbs. parsley
fresh dill
salt and pepper to taste

Chop carrot, beets and celery into small pieces. Simmer with bay leaves in enough water to cover until tender. Add parsley, salt and pepper. Simmer for two more minutes. Serve with chopped dill. For a heartier soup add ½ cup brown rice and an extra cup of water when the vegetables are simmered. Cook until the rice and vegetables are soft.

Carrot Soup

½ lb. carrots, sliced thinly
1 onion, sliced thinly
    (optional)
4 cups vegetable stock or
    water, or 2 cups either stock
    or water and 2 cups nut or
    seed milk.

2 Tbs. oil
½ cup cooked brown rice
½ tsp. dried thyme
½ tsp. kelp
pinch of paprika, nutmeg,
    cinnamon

Add oil to heavy saucepan and heat. Add carrots and onion. Cover and steam 5 minutes. Add stock, rice and seasonings. Cover and simmer for 20 minutes. Put in blender (2 batches). Blend until smooth. Return to saucepan and heat. Good with cashew milk.

DAY FOUR

Cauliflower Soup

1 head cauliflower
3 cups vegetable stock

salt and pepper to taste
watercress

Break up cauliflower into sections. You can make vegetable stock by simmering a mixture of vegetables in water for 30 minutes or use water. Blend cauliflower with stock until it is smooth. Heat for 15 minutes. Add salt and pepper. Garnish with watercress. If you prefer use half cauliflower and half broccoli or cabbage.

NON-ROTATING

Bean Soup

3-½ cups water
2 cups of a mixture of any of
    chopped onion, celery,
    carrots, parsley, turnip,
    potatoes

3 chopped tomatoes
½ tsp. basil, oregano, paprika
¼ tsp. rosemary or salt
1-½ cups cooked or canned
    beans

Bring water to a boil. Add chopped vegetables and herbs. Simmer for 15 minutes. Add cooked beans, e.g. lima, navy, black, soy, pinto, or Romano. Simmer an additional 10 minutes.

Split Pea Soup with Herbs

1 cup dry split peas
4 cups water
1 red pepper
1 small onion

1 carrot
parsley
¼ tsp. chervil
½ tsp. savory

Combine the peas, water and onion and simmer for 45 minutes. Add chopped vegetables and herbs and cook 15 minutes longer. Blend for a smoother texture.

Lentil Soup

1½ cups lentils, washed
1½ quarts cold water
2 Tbs. olive oil
3 cloves garlic, chopped
1 stalk celery, chopped
fresh ground black pepper

1 onion, chopped fine
¼ cup celery leaves, chopped
⅓ cup brown rice or millet
2 Tbs. tomato paste
2 Tbs. parsley, chopped

In heavy pot, heat oil. Add chopped vegetables and rice. Cook, stirring for 5 minutes. Add lentils and water. Bring to a boil, cover and simmer 1½-2 hours. During the last 15 minutes, add chopped kale, escarole or spinach. As an alternative you can mix 1 cup lentils with ½ cup split peas.

Vegetable Soup

2-3 Tbs. oil
1 onion chopped (optional)
4 potatoes diced or 3 sweet
    potatoes diced
4 cups tomato juice, or 3 Tbs.
tomato paste

1 cup chopped parsley or
    chives
4 carrots thinly sliced
2 turnips diced
¼ head cabbage, shredded

Heat oil and saute onion until tender (if using tomato paste, add now and saute). Add potatoes, carrots, turnips, cabbage and ½-1 cup water to cover. Simmer until potatoes and turnip are tender, about ½ hour. Add the tomato juice (or 4 cups water) and continue cooking until heated. Add the chopped parsley or chives and serve.

Beans

Beans are a wonderful alternative to bread and other grains as a side dish. They can be used instead of meats, chicken or cheese for fillings. There are dozens of different beans available. If you are allergic to one type of bean, you may not be allergic to the other types. The bean family includes lentils, chickpeas (garbanzo beans) and peas. Lentils come in many different sizes and colours. When buying lentils examine them before cooking. Often you will find small stones the colour of the lentils. Lentils will cook up much more quickly than other beans. East Indian, Middle eastern, South American and other ethnic cookbooks will have many ideas on how to cook lentils.

To cook any dried bean, soak it overnight first in water. Use three parts of water for each of beans. Discard any floating or discoloured beans. Change the water and simmer until they are tender. Alternatively, you could put the dried beans in a pot with a similar amount of water. Bring to boil and simmer for 5 minutes. Cover and leave for one hour. If still hard, simmer until soft. Canned beans are more expensive but need not be cooked to soften. Simply heat them and use in your recipe. Use any spices or sauces you like with the beans. Tomato sauce, paprika, chili, basil and oregano are all good with beans.

Fava Beans

These are large green beans that you can buy fresh, frozen dried or canned. The pod must not be eaten. Fresh or canned fava beans can be eaten raw or boiled for a few minutes until tender. Add them to soups, stir fries or use as a vegetable with a main dish. They are also called broad beans or fool.

Refried Beans

Saute cooked pinto, Romano, navy, kidney or any other bean in a little oil. Crush them as they heat. Add chili powder to taste and use to stuff tortillas or any vegetable or use as a side dish.

Red Lentils

These are quite small and become paler with cooking. They will cook up very quickly using about two parts water to one part lentils. Infants seem to enjoy very much. They can be combined with any other grain to form patties or add to chopped vegetables to make a loaf.

Fool Nabed

1 cup dried white fava beans	1 large sprig parsley
4 cups water	2-3 large cloves garlic, crushed
⅓ cup lemon juice	or minced
⅓ cup tahini (see page 187)	1-1½ cups garbanzo stock or
1 tsp. salt	water
¼-½ tsp. chili pepper	2 Tbs. oil

Cover fava beans with water. Soak overnight to reduce cooking time. Boil in heavy saucepan over high heat. Cover. Reduce heat to medium low. Simmer until tender. Drain. (Reserve stock for later use.) Remove skins. Mash in food mill, with fork or fingers (not blender) ½ cup at a time. Add the remaining ingredients and mix to a smooth paste. It should be smooth and firm. Chill 2 3 hours or overnight. Pour on top 2 Tbs. oil and sprinkle with chili powder and fresh parsley.

Curried Lentils

1 cup lentils	1 tsp. curry powder
2 cups water	1 Tbs. oil

Cook lentils in water until tender. Heat oil in a skillet. Add curry powder. Heat briefly and add cooked lentils. Mix and simmer 5 minutes

Split Pea Soup

1 cup dry split peas	1 carrot
4 cups water	parsley
1 small onion	2 Tbs. oil

Combine the peas, water and simmer for 45 minutes. Saute chopped onion, carrot and parsley in an oiled pan until soft. If you like a creamy texture blend the cooked peas and water until smooth. Add the sauteed vegetables and cook 15 minutes longer. Take care that it does not burn. Add salt and pepper to taste.

Spicy Dal (Lentil)

1 cup green or red lentils	1/4 tsp. cayenne pepper
8 cups water	1 tsp. cumin see
1/2 tsp. salt	4 whole cloves
2 Tbs. oil	1 tsp. mustard seed
1 tsp. tumeric	

Clean the lentil, looking out for any small stones. Boil water and add lentils. Cook until the lentils are soft. Just about all of the water will have been absorbed. Add the oil to a heated frying pan and add the mustard seed. When it begins to pop add the other spices. Fry for a few minutes and add the cooked lentils. Stir as it come to a boil and serve. Good to accompany vegetables or a main course.

Bean Pate

1 cup Romano or pinto beans	1 tsp. basil
3 cups water	1 tsp. cumin
1 tsp. oil	1/2 tsp. pepper

Soak beans overnight if possible. Drain. Add to boiling water and cook until tender. Add more water if needed. Drain. Pass through grinder or mash thoroughly and mix in spices. Roll into lettuce leaves and serve with alfalfa sprouts and cucumber.

Bean Patties

2 cups cooked or canned
  Romano, soy, pinto or navy
  bean
2-3 Tbs. sesame butter (tahini)
½ tsp. cumin
Oil

½ cup chopped, sauteed and
  drained mushrooms (if
  tolerated)
¼ tsp. pepper
4 Tbs. chickpea flour

Mix all ingredients except flour. Shape into patties and lightly dust with flour. Saute till brown in oiled pan on medium heat. Use garlic and cumin if not rotating.

Lentil Nut Loaf or Patties

3 cups lentils (medium soft
  puree)
½ cup ground pumpkin seeds
1 Tbs. soy sauce or ½ tsp. salt
basil and sage

4 Tbs. oil
1½ cups raw nuts (chopped
  peanuts, cashews)
½ cup chickpeas, cooked or
  canned

Mix all ingredients well. Bake in oiled loaf pan for 1 hour at 350° F. Good with peanut or cashew gravy. Or form into hamburger size patties and bake for 20 to 30 minutes.

Herbed Chickpeas

Saute 1 cup cooked or canned (drained) chickpeas in 2 Tbs. oil. Sprinkle lightly with basil, oregano or rosemary

Vegetarian Dinners

DAY ONE

Tofu Burger

1 pound firm tofu
½ tsp. salt
½ cup grated and drained
   zucchini

½ tsp. basil or oregano
4 large chopped mushrooms if
   tolerated

Blend tofu and salt in blender until smooth. Add zucchini, herbs and mushrooms. Form into patties. Saute in a well oiled pan on medium heat until browned on each side, about two or three minutes.

DAY TWO

Millet Patties

½ onion
½ green pepper
2 cups cooked millet

½ tsp. basil
½ tsp. oregano

Saute chopped onion and green pepper until slightly softened. Beat millet and eggs together until free from lumps. Add the vegetables and herbs. Saute in an oiled pan over medium heat until browned. Turn and saute the second side. Serve with vegetables or with chicken.

Pizza Crust

1 cup chickpea flour
½ cup sweet rice flour (skip rice
   on next rotation cycle)

2 tsp. baking powder
2 Tbs. oil
water as needed-about ½ cup

Sift flours and baking powder together. Add oil and water. Spread out on an oiled cookie sheet. Add toppings and bake at 450° F. until it starts to brown, about 20-30 minutes. Produces a thin crust.

Peruvian Pastel

¼ cup oil
4 cups corn kernels
salt to taste
4 eggs
2 hard boiled eggs

1 onion-diced
2 cloves garlic
1 red or green pepper-diced
1 tomato-diced

Heat the oil in a large saucepan. Puree the corn kernels in a blender. Add to the oil and add salt if desired. Continue cooking over low heat as you beat in the four eggs one at a time. When the mixture has thickened allowed to cool. Hard boil the two eggs and slice in half lengthwise. Saute the onions, garlic, pepper and tomato in a little oil until softened. Oil a deep casserole dish and pour one-third of the egg-corn mixture into the bottom. Let it also coat the sides of the dish. Arrange the sliced eggs on the corn and pour the sauteed vegetables on top. Cover with the rest of the corn-egg mixture. Bake at 350° for about an hour until the egg is set. If you like add cooked chicken to the vegetables.

Quick Millet Loaf

1 cup raw millet
1 cup tomatoes
1 medium onion, cut into
  pieces
½ cup walnuts or pecans
  (optional)
1 tsp. Italian seasoning

2 cups water
1 tsp. salt
1 can black olives, quartered
2 finely chopped sun-dried
  tomatoes (optional)

Put millet into casserole. Blend together tomatoes, onion, nuts and water. Add blender ingredients and remaining ingredients to millet. Mix. Bake at 325° F. for 2 hours. If too dry add more water and bake till water is absorbed. Millet can be cooked in advance in which case bake only 25 minutes.

Cornmeal/Polenta

1 cup cornmeal   4 cups cold water

Add cornmeal to water and bring to boil while stirring. Cook about 30 minutes stirring frequently and pour into an oiled 8x14 inch pan. Top with fish in tomato sauce (see page 131), spicy sauteed vegetables or any other topping. If not rotating try beans or meat sauce.

French Corn Cakes

2 cups corn kernels (fresh, frozen or canned)	⅓ cup corn flour
3 eggs	dash of salt
2 Tbs. oil	

Cook fresh or frozen corn. Drain canned corn. Puree all ingredients in a blender. Heat a large heavy frying pan. Add oil and pour out small 2½ inch rounds of batter. Press down lightly with a fork. Cook until starting to brown, flip and cook the other side.

Corn Tamales

4 cups canned, fresh or frozen corn kernels	dash salt
¾ cup chopped onions (optional)	½ tsp. chili powder
1 cup chopped tomatoes	2 Tbs. chopped scallions or green pepper
	2 Tbs. oil

Drain canned corn. Mix all ingredients together. Cut out 12, 6 inch aluminum foil squares. Place part of the mixture in the centre of each square. Roll up foil and twist the ends to seal it securely. Cook in boiling water for 45 minutes. Drain and serve. Serves six.

Ratatouille (Vegetable Stew)

1 onion, chopped
2 cloves garlic, chopped
¼ cup parsley or chives,
   chopped
1 eggplant, cut in 2 inch cubes
1-2 green peppers, in chunks
1 tsp. basil

pinch of salt
2-3 leeks, sliced with greens
¼ cup olive oil
pinch of red or black pepper
2 Tbs. tomato paste mixed in ½
   cup water
3 ripe tomatoes, chopped

Saute onion and garlic in oil. Add the rest of the ingredients. Put on a tight fitting lid and cook on low to medium heat for ½ hour. Vegetables cook in their own juice so don't lift the lid too often.

Tacos

Frozen or packaged tortillas or taco shells can be lightly baked or fried. Roll up with avocado, tomato, onion, green pepper, chicken, egg slices or whatever else you fancy.

DAY THREE

Nasi Goreng

1 cup brown rice
2 cups water
4 Tbs. oil
1 carrot

2 stalks celery
¼ tsp. shrimp or fish paste
½ cup hazelnuts (optional)
½ cup shrimp (optional)

Add rice to boiling water and cook until all of water is absorbed. Cut carrot into thin slices or 2 inch long thin strands. Cut celery into thin slices. Chop hazelnuts coarsely. Add 2 Tbs. oil to heated frying pan and saute carrot and celery with shrimp paste until soft. Add shrimp and continue cooking until it is done. Add hazelnuts and cook for 2 more minutes. Add rest of oil to vegetables, add rice and mix. Cook for five more minutes and serve.

Wild Rice Ring

1 cup wild rice	¼ cup oil
4 cups boiling water	½ tsp. basil or parsley

Wash the rice and cook it without stirring until tender. Add herbs and oil. Place the rice in an oiled 7 inch ring mould. Place in a pan of hot water and bake at 350° F. for 20 minutes. Carefully empty the ring onto a platter. You can fill the centre with shrimp or lamb.

DAY FOUR

Kasha Loaf - non-egg

See Kasha loaf below but omit egg and use cabbage or broccoli rather than carrot and onion.

Apple-Sweet Potato Casserole

2 pounds sweet potatoes or yams	¼ tsp. nutmeg
½ cup oil	2 medium cooking apples

Steam sweet potatoes until soft. Mash and add oil. Peel and thinly slice the apples. Oil a baking dish and place apple slices over the surface. Sprinkle with nutmeg. Place mashed sweet potatoes on top. Bake at 350° for 45 minutes. For dinner serve with buckwheat kasha.

NON-ROTATING RECIPES

Chickpea Patties

28 oz. can chickpeas	1 leek
1 large carrot	1 egg or ¼ cup soft tofu

Grate carrot and chop leek. Steam both until soft. Blend with the drained chickpeas in a food processor or mash into a reasonably smooth paste. Form into patties and fry. Turn when browned. Makes 7 patties.

Tofu Casserole

1 lb. soft tofu in ½ inch cubes
½ cup peas
1 zucchini, thinly sliced
½ tsp. kelp, dulse or salt

1 cup tomato sauce
1 onion, chopped
1 clove garlic, chopped

Saute tofu, zucchini, onion and garlic. Place in casserole and pour on the tomato sauce. Cover and cook at 375° F. for 20 minutes.

Kasha (buckwheat groats) Loaf

2¾ cups water
½ cup grated carrot
1⅓ cups kasha
½ cup oat flour

paprika
1 Tbs. chopped onion
1 clove minced onion
1 egg-beaten

Saute onion and garlic in oil. Boil the water, then add carrots, kasha, onion and garlic. Cover. Reduce heat and cook for 20 minutes. Mix in the egg and flour. Pour into an oiled casserole and bake 30 minutes at 350° F. Serve with hot tomato sauce or nut gravy, sprinkled with paprika.

Yam/Sweet Potato Pie

2 lb. yams or sweet potato
1 cup canned unsweetened
    pineapple

2 Tbs. lemon juice
¼ cup raisins (optional)
½ tsp. cinnamon (optional)

Steam yams until soft and peel. Mash to fine texture with other ingredients. Serve cold or reheat covered in oven.

Vegetables

Jerusalem Artichokes

These starchy roots are crisp and mildly sweet when eaten raw and can be added to fresh green salads. They can be used in place of potatoes or water chestnuts in any recipe or add to your favourite stir fry recipe. They can be used as a substitute for potatoes in soups and stews. Steam them and serve with oil or a sauce. They can be baked, mashed or microwaved. One pound will take about 5-6 minutes in a covered dish. They can be made into chips by slicing them thinly and baking them like the potato chips on page 122. Wash and scrape them thoroughly to remove dirt from the crevices. Do not freeze or cook them in an iron pot. Store in a ventilated plastic bag in the refrigerator. If they have lost crispness, freshen by soaking in ice water.

Jicama

Jicama is a crisp, large, white fleshed root vegetable with a thin brown skin. It can be used in salads and cooking to replace apples or water chestnuts. It can be sliced into sticks and served raw, perhaps sprinkled with salt, cayenne or lemon juice.

Plantain

Plantains are a large yellow, red, black or green skinned banana-like vegetable. Unlike banana it must be cooked before eating. A green plantain is not ripe but will ripen soon if kept at room temperature. When green they are very difficult to peel. Before cooking, peel and remove any fibres. Cut in half lengthwise and saute each side in an oiled pan until lightly browned. You could also score one side of the plantain and bake in a 350° oven for thirty to forty five minutes until soft.

Baked Squash

Cut squash into halves. Bake face up at 375°F. for 1 hour, or until very soft. Add a little cinnamon or honey if desired. Serve with a salad.

Sprouts

Sprouted seeds and beans are very rich sources of nutrients. The sprouts may contain higher levels of vitamins than the seeds that they were sprouted from. Infants who can eat soft foods and older children all like to eat these long stranded sprouts. They seem to appeal to children just as noodles do. All sprouts can be eaten raw and the more firm and large types such as mung and soy bean sprouts can be lightly cooked. They can be added to soups, salads and appetizers. Many different types of sprouts can be purchased at supermarkets or natural food stores. You can also sprout your own with very little trouble.

To grow sprouts, first select fresh, good quality seeds of alfalfa, radish, lentils, soy beans, peas, chickpeas, sunflower seeds or mung beans. Indeed any grain can be sprouted. Wash one-half cup of seeds. It will grow into a quart of sprouts. Soak for about 8 hours in ample lukewarm water. There are two methods to use next.
1. Place the soaked seeds in a glass covered casserole dish and put in a warm, dark place. Rinse thoroughly at least twice a day.
2. Place the seeds in a large mouth quart jar. Cover the mouth with cheese cloth or a fine mesh covering. Soak the seeds three times a day and then turn the jar over to drain the seeds thoroughly. Then place the jar in a warm, dark place on its side.

The most flavour comes from sprouts at these lengths: alfalfa, 1-2 inches, mung beans, 2-3 inches, soy bean, 1-3 inches, wheat and sunflower, when the same length as the seed, lentil. 1 inch. Lentil sprouts mould more easily than others. When the sprouts are ready, refrigerate them in a closed jar and use within a few days. Radish sprouts have a tangy flavour.

Tofu/Bean Curd

Tofu or bean curd is the coagulated protein component of soy beans. Tofu is manufactured by boiling soy beans and then adding magnesium chloride or calcium chloride (nigiri) to the liquid which causes coagulation. There is no mould or fermentation used in the process. It is usually purchased in small blocks. These blocks may be very soft or quite firm. Soft tofu is useful for making spreads, deserts or any recipe where the tofu is blended. Firmer tofu will stand up to stir frying or cooking in casseroles. Tofu is also available in dried sheets. These can be added to soups or stews or softened in water and used to wrap foods before cooking. Tofu itself has a very mild, bland flavour, but it will take on any flavours in the foods or sauces with which it is cooked. Infants enjoy eating the semi-firm tofu. They can pick up chunks of it and feed themselves. Since it is soft it requires no teeth.

Zucchini

Slice a washed zucchini into ½ inch chunks or ¼ inch slices. Lightly fry zucchini chunks in sunflower oil with sweet basil or oregano.

DAY TWO

Lotus Root

This is the root of the lotus or water lily plant. It is about four to six inches long and two to three inches wide with a brown surface. When you cut into it you will see that it has many hollow areas that give it a snowflake pattern. It is available fresh or canned. Peel the fresh root and cut into slices. The slices can be deep fried or made into chips like the Potato/Taro Chips below. It can also be stir fried or used in a recipe to replace potato where a firm vegetable is needed.

Taro

Peel off the thick brown skin. The white flesh will turn red if exposed to air. Cut into small pieces and cook as you would a potato, however it will take longer to cook. It is good in a vegetable or meat stew.

Potato/Taro Chips

Slice potatoes or taro as thinly as possible. Place on an oiled cookie sheet in a single layer. Broil until done, about 15 minutes. Turn and broil the other side. Be careful as they burn easily when done. If you like sprinkle with basil, hot pepper or other herbs before broiling.

Sesame Scalloped Potatoes

Chopped onions
1 tsp. basil
sliced potatoes
½ cubed green or red pepper

1 Tbs. parsley
1 quart sesame milk (see page 68)

Slice scrubbed potatoes into casserole dish until half full. Add a layer of chopped onions and pepper. Add 1 tsp. basil and 1 Tbs. chopped parsley. Completely fill the casserole with sliced potatoes and add enough unstrained sesame milk to cover, approximately 1 quart. Bake at 425°F. for 1 hour or until soft.

Seaweeds

Although not very well known in European cooking, seaweeds are a very nutritious and flavourful part of many maritime oriental cultures. The many different types of seaweed have different flavours, consistencies and appearances. Seaweeds are particularly high in trace mineral content. The following suggestions will introduce you to some of them.

Arame and Hijiki

All children and infants love long stringy noodles. Arame and hijiki are black seaweeds in the form of noodles. They are prepared and packaged in a dry and crisp form. Before using, they need to be soaked or cooked until soft. Hijiki will need more time than arame but is firmer and more like spaghetti. Arame has a milder, sweeter taste but may be too stringy for easy eating. Infants who can chew soft foods will love to grasp the strands and feed themselves.

Nori

Nori is packaged in sheets. Often it is roasted before packaging. It can be eaten right out of the package as a snack or can be crumbled into soups, stews or any dish. It has a mild flavour. It is traditionally used to roll up rice into sushi or maki.

Dulse and Kelp

These are often available in powder form. They can be used like salt to add extra flavour at the table or while cooking. Kelp has a stronger flavour and should be used in small amounts initially. Dulse is a red colour and is also available dried and whole. It makes an interesting and slightly salty snack for munching right out of the bag.

Kombu

Kombu is black and comes in long strips. It, like any of the other seaweeds, can be used to make a flavourful soup broth by soaking in cold water for 3-4 hours. Then make your soup with the liquid. It can also be added to soups, stews, beans, casseroles or grains as they cook. Infants will enjoy chewing on pieces of the strips when they have been softened with cooking.

Agar Agar

This is not a misprint. Agar agar is a seaweed that can be used as a substitute for gelatin. It can be used to thicken foods or to make a jelly. It is colourless and flavourless but stiffer than gelatin. In Japan it is called kanten. To use agar agar, sprinkle the flakes with a little cold water to soften it and after a few minutes heat with water. Do not boil too long or it will lose its thickness. One teaspoon will thicken about 1 cup of liquid.

Grape Leaves

Grape leaves are available bottled, canned or fresh. Rinse preserved leaves to remove brine and then use. Fresh leaves will need to be steamed for a minute before use. Use them to wrap fillings such as grains, lentils or minced meats. Place them shiny side down. Place a small amount of filling in the centre of the leaf and then roll up the sides.

DAY THREE

Water Chestnuts

This tuber of an aquatic plant is about the size and shape of a peeled chestnut. It has a crisp refreshing flavour when fresh. They are fresh available in the summer and fall and also canned. Peel fresh water chestnuts and eat them raw or slice and simmer for two minutes. You could also cook them whole until tender or use them in stir fries. They are a wonderful alternative to potato.

Cassava

Cassava, also called manioc, is a starchy root vegetable cultivated in South America and Africa. It is the source of tapioca and is often used in the form of a flour called gari.

Gari can be cooked into a bland porridge. Heat 1 ⅔ cup water to boiling, remove from heat and stir in the gari with rapid strokes. Stir until it is quite thick. Pour into a small bowl and serve immediately. It is best to use this with flavourful accompaniments.

Frozen cassava can be boiled for 30 to 45 minutes until tender and then served. Fresh cassava should be peeled and washed. Cut into one to two inch sections and boil for an hour or more. Drain and remove stringy parts. Mash or dice and serve. Raw cassava is toxic and must be thoroughly cooked before eating.

Carrots Vichy

Place in saucepan:

2 cups scraped, sliced carrots	1 Tbs. oil
½ cup boiling water	1 Tbs. lemon juice
1 Tbs. sweetener (optional)	

Cover the pan tightly. Cook over quick heat until water evaporates. Let brown in the oil. Serve sprinkled with chives or parsley.

Parsnips

Peel, then cut in half 4 medium sized parsnips. Place in oiled, ovenproof dish. Add 2 Tbs. oil. Sprinkle with ¼ tsp. salt. Add to dish ¾ cup stock or water. Cover and bake until tender, approximately 45 minutes. Or prepare as for Carrots Vichy.

Spinach and Swiss Chard

Spinach and swiss chard, also called silverbeet, can be useful and versatile additions to your diet. After thoroughly washing and rinsing them, place them in a large pot with some washing water still clinging to the leaves. Cook over moderate heat until they just start to wilt. Drain and eat. Or you could heat some oil, perhaps with garlic if not rotating. Perhaps add ¼ cup of rice cracker crumbs. Press the liquid out of the greens, a potato ricer works well, chop into small pieces and saute briefly.

DAY FOUR

Arrowroot

Arrowroot is the tuber of a tropical plant. It has a slightly sweet flavour and a grainy texture. It has a long, thin rootlike appearance. Boil it until tender and then after peeling serve as a potato. The Chinese call it chok wa. The flour has many uses as a thickener and binder in recipes.

Bamboo Shoots

These are exactly what they seem to be. The young shoots of the bamboo plant. They are crisp and creamy in colour. You will find them available either fresh in season in Asian markets or canned. To cook fresh bamboo shoots remove the outside husk and then boil for fifteen minutes. Rinse and slice. Then use them in stir-fried vegetable, stews or anywhere you want a firm vegetable. Try them in salads.

Baked Red Cabbage

1 medium red cabbage	¼ cup dried apples - diced
1 cooking apple	(optional)

Cut the red cabbage into thin pieces. Slice or dice the apple and mix with the cabbage. Add the dried apples. Place in an oiled casserole dish. Cover and bake at 350° for about 45 minutes or until the cabbage is tender.

Yams/Sweet Potato

Both of these starchy roots come in a variety of sizes and colours, yams are darker and sweeter. These are technically separate species and true yams are seldom found in North America. They are often confused and mislabelled in stores. They are not related to white potato and are an excellent substitute. They can be baked, steamed, mashed or used in any potato recipe.

Sweet Potato-Baked

Scrub and bake at 425° for 40-60 minutes or steam until soft (about 25 minutes). Micro-wave small sweet potatos for about 5 minutes. Serve with cabbage salad (see below) or cooked cabbage.

Sweet Potato Pie

5 sweet potatoes or yams
1½ cups ground almonds
1 tsp. nutmeg

1 tsp. allspice
¼ cup maple syrup (optional)
1 tsp. cinnamon

Steam sweet potatoes until tender. Peel and mash or whip thoroughly. Add the other ingredients except almonds. Spread almonds onto pie plate, add sweet potatoes and bake at 375° F. for 40 minutes. Good hot or cold. If not rotating, add ½ cup pineapple chunks.

NON-ROTATING RECIPES

Swiss Chard Pie

6 large chard leaves
1 potato
1 onion
1 zucchini

1 clove garlic
4 eggs or 10 oz. soft tofu
½ tsp. basil

Cut the chard into small pieces and steam until soft. Chop the potato into small pieces and steam until soft. Chop the zucchini and onion. Saute with the garlic until softened. Blend the tofu or beat the eggs and combine with all of the chard, potato, zucchini and basil. Pour into a well oiled pie plate and bake at 350° until done, about an hour.

Fruit

DAY ONE

Carob (St. John's bread)

Carob is the pod of a large middle eastern tree. It is sometimes available whole. It can be eaten like a very hard candy bar since it is quite sweet. Watch out for the small hard seeds. It is usually available in powdered form and can be used as a substitute for chocolate although it does not taste exactly like chocolate. A little nutmeg will give it more of a chocolate flavour. Carob syrup made from the pods is very, very sweet. It is available in middle eastern food stores.

Durian

This is a large spiky fruit from south-east Asia. It has a soft centre with a taste like strawberry custard. It also has a very strong smell that some people find unpleasant. It is served raw.

Jackfruit

Another large fruit from south-east Asia. It is available canned and sometimes fresh and is eaten raw when ripe or cooked like a vegetable when unripe.

DAY TWO

Custard Apple/Cherimoya

This is a apple sized, green, scale covered fruit with a very soft, sweet, white interior. It has a lovely indescribable flavour. It is eaten raw but watch for the many seeds.

Persimmon

Two varities of persimmons are often available in the fall. The type with a pointed bottom are allowed to ripen until very soft. The fruit can be cut in half and the pulp eaten with a spoon. The skin is very astringent and not pleasant to eat. The other variety has a flat bottom, more tomato shaped. It can be eaten whole like an apple or sliced into segments.

DAY THREE

Litchi, Longan, Rambutan

These three fruits are very similar with a firm outer skin, a juicy white fruit and a large central seed. The rambutan has a spiky red shell, the others are rough and brown. The flavour is very sweet and delicious. They are available fresh or canned and are eaten raw.

Mangosteen

Inside of a thick purple skin are succulent, sweet, white sections. It comes from south-east Asia and is eaten raw.

DAY FOUR

Starfruit (Carambola)

This is a small yellow-green fruit that is star shaped in cross-section. It has a waxy exterior and has sour taste. It can be eaten raw or juiced.

Fish, Meat and Fowl

Fish Sauces

Pour one of these sauces on broiled or baked fish.

Ginger Sauce
Simmer ¼ cup oil (or butter) with the juice and finely grated peel of 1 orange, 1 tsp. grated fresh ginger and 1 small clove of garlic for 5 minutes.

Herb Sauce
Blend ¼ cup olive oil with 1 tsp. Dijon mustard, 1 Tbs. lemon juice and pinch of cayenne. Add 1 Tbs. chopped fresh dill or tarragon.

Tomato Caper Sauce

28 oz. canned tomatoes   1 Tbs. capers
2 cloves garlic   ¼ tsp. oregano
¼ tsp. basil

Puree or chop drained tomatoes. Simmer in a saucepan with crushed garlic, drained capers and oregano and basil until it begins to thicken slightly.

DAY ONE

Broiled White Fish

Fish should be cleaned, with or without head. Rub both sides of fish with oil and pepper if desired. Place in an oiled pan and broil until brown. Flip and broil the other side. Use these instructions with any large fish such as salmon or trout.

Salmon

Sliced smoked salmon or B.B.Q. tidbits can be eaten for breakfast or lunch. Eat alone or with the biscuits below. Great high protein meal.

Salmon Salad

Herbed Salad
Use tinned or left over salmon. Mix 7 oz. salmon thoroughly with 2 Tbs. oil and herbs (basil, oregano etc.) to taste.

Mayonnaise Salad
Mix 7 oz. salmon with 2 Tbs. soy mayonnaise (see Gravies and Dressings) and serve on leaves of lettuce.

Roast Beef

Pre-heat oven to 450°. Trim off fat closely and place rib roast in oven. Turn down to 350° and cook 18-20 minutes per pound. One pound gives 3-4 servings. Use leftovers for other meals served on lettuce or chickpea biscuits.

DAY TWO

Fish in Tomato Sauce

1 small onion chopped	¼ tsp. thyme
1 clove chopped garlic	¼ tsp. marjoram
¼ tsp. sage	¼ cup 32 oz. can of tomatoes
¼ tsp. kelp	or 4-5 fresh peeled tomatoes
2 Tbs. oil	1½ lbs. of fish- cod, haddock
1 chili pepper	

Saute the chopped small onion in 2 Tbs. oil. Add spices and herbs. Add 32 oz. tin of tomatoes (or 4 fresh) pureed or chopped fine. Simmer for ½ hour. Add fish cut into 2 inch pieces. Simmer for 10 minutes. Serve over millet - see page 88, or over polenta - see page 115.

Millet Primavera

6½ cups chicken stock
2 cups millet
2¼ cups in total of chopped
   red and green peppers,
   asparagus tips, leeks or firm
   tomatoes

¼ cup minced onion
½-1 cup cubed chicken
   (optional)
¼ cup oil
2 Tbs. oil

Bring the chicken stock to a boil. In a deep heavy pan saute the onion in oil. Add the millet to the onion and stir for one minute. Add ½ cups of the boiling chicken stock and stir until the liquid is absorbed. Briefly saute the chicken and add to the millet. Add 1 cup more of the stock and repeat. Add the vegetables and 1 cup more of the stock. When this broth has been absorbed add the rest of the stock one cup at a time until all the broth is absorbed. Add 2 Tbs. oil, mix with two forks and serve.

Seafood Paella

2 cups water
2 cups canned or fresh
   tomatoes
2 cups millet
1 large onion
4 cloves garlic
¼ cup oil

1 red pepper
pinch saffron
½ tsp. basil
1 pound cod, haddock or
   mullet fillets
¼ tsp. cayenne (optional)

Combine the water and sliced tomatoes in a large pot, heat to boiling and add the washed millet. Slice the onion, dice the garlic and saute in the oil until the onion starts to become transparent. Slice the pepper in long strips and saute for 2 minutes. Add to the cooking millet. Cut the fish into 1 inch squares. When the water is almost all absorbed add the saffron, basil and fish. If the millet is not quite cooked add more water or tomato juice. Serve while hot. It will keep refrigerated overnight and can be reheated the next day.

Cod or Carp

Both are available smoked and make a good, quick breakfast or lunchserved with tortillas

Chicken/Avocado Tostada

Bake or fry tortillas until crisp. Apply a thin layer of mayonnaise. Top with generous layers of cooked chicken and/or avocado, tomato, green onions, green peppers. Top with hot chiles or hot chile sauce.

DAY THREE

Red Snapper

Bake, broil or poach. Bake covered for 10 minutes per 1 inch thickness or until flaky. Broil eachside 4 inches from heat watching for burning. Poach on a steamer for about 10 minutes.

Baked Red Snapper

2 rice cakes	*½ tsp. basil*
½ tsp. parsley	*½ pound red snapper fillets*

Use the small, square, crisp rice cakes available in natural food stores. Grind them in a blender or mortar until they are form a fine crumb. Add the parsley and basil. Mix these together and coat both side of the snapper fillets with the mixture. Bake at 350° for 15 to 20 minutes until the fish separates easily when a fork is inserted. Use this recipe for any fish fillet that is available. Makes one serving.

Lamb

Broil lamb chops 4 inches from heat on both sides till done, or use minced lamb to make lamb patties as you would with beef. Serve with rice crackers and steamed carrots.

Herring, Sardine

Pickled herring or canned sardines with rice cakes make a quick breakfast or lunch.

Fish

Poach, bake or broil, snapper, blue fish or yellow perch. Bake covered for 10 minutes per each inch of thickness or until flaky.

DAY FOUR

Roast Rabbit

1 whole rabbit, cleaned	*1 tsp. rosemary*
oil	*black pepper*

Brush the rabbit with oil. Sprinkle with rosemary and pepper to taste. Preheat the oven to 450° and place the rabbit on its side on a rack in a roasting pan. Reduce heat to 350°. Turn the rabbit after 45 minutes. Baste with oil or drippings every 20 minutes. Continue to cook until tender which will be in about another 45 minutes. Rabbit tastes very much like dark chicken meat.

Roast Pork

Preheat oven to 450°F. Trim fat closely and place pork loin fat side up in pan. Reduce heat to 350° and cook 30-35 minutes per pound. Serve with applesauce. One pound serves 3-4.

Fish

Bake, broil or poach sole, halibut, flounder or ocean perch. See page 134.

Mackerel

Mackerel is available tinned like sardines. Spread onto oat crackers with watercress. Good also for breakfast.

Ham

Slice with apple sauce or olives on oat or buckwheat crackers (see cracker recipes).

NON-ROTATING

Tagine-Moroccan Lamb Stew

1 Tbs. oil	1 small turnips
½ cup chopped celery	½ cup raisins
1 onion chopped	½ 10 oz. can chickpeas
1 pound stewing lamb	2 Tbs. parsley
1 19 oz. can plum tomatoes	⅛ tsp. cayenne
3 inch cinnamon stick	pinch saffron
1 acorn squash	1 red bell pepper
3 carrots	2 small zucchini

Heat the oil and brown the lamb with the celery and onion for five minutes. Bring the tomatoes to a simmer and add the lamb mixture. Add the cinnamon stick. Cut all the vegetables into ½ inch pieces. Add the squash, carrots, turnips, raisins and chickpeas to the lamb. When the lamb is almost cooked add the parsley, cayenne, saffron, peppers and zucchini. Serve on a bed of rice, millet, buckwheat kasha, amaranth or quinoa. Any of the vegetables may be omitted and substituted with vegetables of similar texture. Chuck beef may be used instead of lamb.

Dips, Sauces, Gravies and Dressings

DAY TWO

Guacamole

1 cup mashed avocado
1/3 cup chopped tomato
  (optional)
1 Tbs. chopped onion
  (optional)
1 garlic clove, crushed

1 tsp. water with
  1/4 tsp. ascorbic acid
2 tsp. chopped parsley
chopped hot peppers or
  cayenne pepper to taste

Blend all ingredients together to a fine consistency. Serve with corn chips. (See recipe page 60)

NON-ROTATING

Sesame Gravy

2 cups sesame milk (see
  page 68)

2 Tbs. oil
2 Tbs. potato flour

Combine oil and milk. Stir in flour and slowly heat. Add any herb or spice that you like such as basil, thyme, dill, cayenne or black pepper. Simmer in sauce pan until thick.

Cranberry Sauce

1 cup orange juice
1 small unpeeled apple sliced

1/2-1 cup cooked cranberries
1-2 Tbs. honey

Blend together the juice, apples and honey. Add the cranberries until the mixture thickens.

Baba Ghannouj (Eggplant Sesame Paste Dip)

1 large or 2 small eggplants

Cut off the tip of the eggplant. Bake at 350° F. for 20-30 minutes until soft all over and partly collapsed. Cool. Remove skin. Place in bowl. Mash with fork, food mill or electric egg beater until smooth paste.

Add:

⅓ cup lemon juice
3-4 Tbs. stock or water
6 Tbs. tahini (see page 187)

2-3 large cloves of garlic (crushed or minced)
½ tsp. salt (optional)

Mix to a smooth paste. Add liquid as needed to thin dip. Chill 2-3 hours or overnight.

Topping:

2 Tbs. olive oil
1 sprig parsley

¼ tsp. chili pepper

Serve with green peppers, carrots, celery or other crisp vegetables.

Vegetable Walnut Pate

1½ cups green beans
2 eggs
¼ cup toasted walnuts
2 Tbs. mayonnaise

½ cup finely minced onion
2 Tbs. dry white wine (if tolerated)

Blend separately green beans and walnuts. Saute the onion. Combine and mix finely all the ingredients. Season with salt, pepper, and nutmeg as desired.

Humus (Chickpea-Sesame Paste Dip)

1 cup chickpeas (garbanzos)   *4 cups water*

Cover chickpeas with water. Soak overnight to reduce cooking time. Boil in heavy saucepan over high heat. Cover. Reduce heat to medium low. Simmer until tender. Drain. (Reserve stock for later use.) Mash with food mill, fork or fingers (not blender) ½ cup at a time. Then add:

⅓ cup lemon juice	*1 large sprig parsley*
¼ cup sesame butter (tahini)	*2-3 large cloves garlic, minced*
1 tsp. salt	*½ cups chickpea stock*
¼-½ tsp. chili pepper ground	*2 Tbs. olive or vegetable oil*

Mix to smooth paste. Should have dip consistency. Chill 2-3 hours or overnight.

Topping:
2 Tbs. oil	*1 large sprig parsley*
¼-½ tsp. chili pepper	

Before serving sprinkle with any of the toppings.

Nut Gravies

2 cups of cashew or nut milk	*2 Tbs. arrowroot powder*
2 Tbs. chopped onion	*pinch of sea salt*
2 Tbs. oil (optional)	

Combine all of the above and season with a pinch of either basil, thyme, dill, celery seed powder, garlic, cayenne or black pepper. Simmer in saucepan until thick. ½ cup of chopped parsley, chives, leeks or alfalfa sprouts may be added prior to serving.

Soy Mayonnaise

½ cup soy or cashew milk   ¼ tsp. celery seed
1 tsp. honey   ½ tsp. paprika
¼ tsp. salt   ⅔ cup soy oil
½ tsp. onion powder   3 Tbs. lemon juice

Blend all ingredients except oil and lemon together. Gradually add oil, very slowly until it becomes thick. Lastly stir in the lemon juice.

Tofu Mayonnaise

1 cup tofu (6½ oz)   pinch of mustard or cayenne
2 Tbs. chopped onion   1 tsp. honey
3 Tbs. lemon juice   ¼ cup oil
paprika or dill to taste

Blend all ingredients except oil and lemon juice. Add oil very slowly while continuing to blend. Add lemon juice, blend 10 seconds more. Good as a dip as well.

Tahini and Honey Syrup

¼ cup honey   ¼ cup tahini

Blend honey and tahini. Add water until it reaches desired thickness. ½ tsp. vanilla is optional. Serve on fruit salad or grains as thick sauce or thin syrup.

Salads

DAY ONE

Sprout Salad

1 cup bean or lentil sprouts   *½ cup thinly sliced cucumbers*
1 cup alfalfa sprouts

Rinse sprouts to remove any seeds. Separate the sprouts fluffing them up and add cucumbers. Add a dressing such as oil and vinegar or tofu salad dressing.

Dandelion Salad

Pick the young soft leaves from garden dandelions. It may be best to avoid dandelions growing near busy streets or where they may have been sprayed. They become bitter and tough if too large and after flowering. Use tofu dressing.

Lettuce Salad

Wash, tear and drain romaine or other leaf lettuce. Add flaked salmon, cucumber, alfalfa sprouts, lentil sprouts. Toss with 1 Tbs. oil per serving (see Gravies and Dressings for other dressings).

Chickpea Salad

To 1 cup cooked or canned chickpeas add 7 oz. of canned artichoke hearts. Add dressing or oil and ¼ tsp. paprika, ¼ tsp. basil, ¼ tsp. oregano to chickpeas.

DAY TWO

Greek Salad

1 tomato
1 green or red pepper
½ Spanish onion

small bunch New Zealand
spinach (if available)

Slice the tomato into small wedges and the pepper into ½ inch squares. Slice the onion thinly and separate the sections. Toss with New Zealand spinach and dress with oil and vinegar. Walnut oil has a wonderful flavour. Use oregano or basil vinegar if you have made it in advance.

Asparagus Salad

1 dozen asparagus tips

½ red pepper

Steam the tips until they are tender. Allow them to cool. Add diced red pepper. Serve on a bed of New Zealand spinach if available. Dress with oil and vinegar.

DAY THREE

Spinach Salad

1 bunch spinach
3 Tbs. parsley sprigs

¼ cup water chestnuts

Thoroughly wash and spin dry the spinach. If using canned water chestnuts, dip in boiling water to remove the can flavour. If using fresh, peel and slice thinly. Use lemon or orange juice and oil dressing.

Carrot Salad

Mandarin Carrot Salad

2 large carrots   *¼ cup orange juice*
2 mandarin oranges

Grate the carrot. Separate the mandarin orange sections. Mix carrot with the mandarins and juice. Chill and serve.

Cooked Carrot Salad
Slice carrots thinly and steam until soft. Toss with oil and lemon juice dressing (See Gravies and Dressings) using dill instead of mustard.

Shrimp and Spinach Salad

Wash, drain, and tear spinach. Wash shelled, cooked shrimp; drain and add to spinach. Top with pine nuts and oil and lemon juice dressing (see Dressing and Gravies). Use 1 Tbs. per serving.

Beet Salad

Steam beets until soft. Peel and slice into ¼ inch wide pieces, let cool and add a lemon and oil dressing (¼ cup oil and 3 Tbs. lemon juice).

Beet and Swiss Chard Salad

Steam whole beets. Peel and slice them thinly. Add cooked, drained, chopped Swiss chard or spinach. Toss with oil that has been warmed in small pan with sliced garlic clove. Do not overheat oil. Add lemon juice if desired.

Citrus Fruit Salad

Separate sections of oranges, grapefruit, tangerine. Serve with coconut milk. Top with coconut, ground hazelnuts or sunflower seeds.

DAY FOUR

Cole Slaw

½ cup cabbage
4 radishes

1 eating apple

Cut the cabbage into small pieces. Add finely chopped radish and the apple cut into thin wedges. Dress with olive oil. Try this also with Chinese cabbage (sui choy).

Tuna Salad

Mix a can of tuna with sliced olives or radishes and a tablespoon olive oil. Serve on oat crackers or rolled into soft cabbage leaves. Good for a quick breakfast.

Red Cabbage Salad

3 Tbs. oil
1 red cabbage, thinly sliced
1 apple, diced
3 Tbs. lemon juice (optional, or
  1 tsp. Vitamin C powder)

1 Tbs. maple syrup (optional)
handful of currants
¼ tsp. allspice
2 whole cloves
dash of nutmeg (optional)

Heat oil in skillet and add cabbage. Cook, stirring until cabbage wilts. Add rest of ingredients. Cook, covered for 15 minutes at low heat.

Plum and Pear Salad

2 cups sliced pears   *3 cups plum chunks*

Mix together with maple syrup or sweetener if desired. Serve with thick almond milk.

NON-ROTATING RECIPES

Sweet Potato Salad

2 sweet potatoes or yams   *2 mandarin oranges*
½ cup celery   *½ cup mayonnaise*
2 Tbs. green onion

Steam the sweet potatoes and dice. Chop the celery and green onions. Combine the vegetables with the separated mandarins and mayonnaise. If you like add chopped roasted nuts.

Peruvian Quinoa Salad

1 cup quinoa   *¼ cup raisins*
2 cups boiling water   *pepper*
½ cup dices red or yellow pepper   *cayenne pepper*
1 cup scallions   *¼ oil*
¼ cup broken pecans   *2 Tbs. lime or lemon juice*

Cook the quinoa in the water until it is absorbed. Cool it and add the vegetables, pecans and raisins. Combine lime juice and oil and pour over the salad.

Salad Dressings

DAY ONE

Tofu Mayonnaise

3 Tbs. distilled white vinegar
  or herb vinegar
  (see page 147, 148)

1 cup tofu (6 oz.)
¼ cup oil

Blend tofu until it is smooth. Add oil very slowly while continuing to blend. Add lemon juice, blend 10 seconds more. Good also as a dip.

Cashew Gravy

2 cups cashew milk (see
  page 67)
2 Tbs. oil

2 Tbs. chickpea flour
¼ tsp. salt

Heat oil and add flour. Cook briefly till flour is browned. Slowly add cashew milk. Add any herb or spice that you like such as basil, thyme, dill, cayenne or black pepper. Simmer in sauce pan until thick.

DAY TWO

Sesame Salad Dressing

¼ cup tahini
1 tsp. kelp
½ clove garlic, finely chopped

juice of ½ lemon
water (to thin dressing)

Combine tahini with kelp, garlic and lemon juice. Add a few tablespoons water to thin to desired thickness. Mix until smooth.

Mock Tuna Spread

To the above recipe add ½ cup chopped onion, ½ cup chopped celery, and ½ cup mixed alfalfa, mung and lentil sprouts. Blend until smooth.

Sesame Butter Dressing

¼ cup sesame butter (tahini)   3 Tbs. lemon juice
1 tsp. grated onion   ¼ tsp. salt
1 tsp. basil   1 Tbs. olive oil

Mix well. Serve over Spring Dandelion Salad or other salads.

DAY THREE

Oil and Lemon Juice Dressing

3 Tbs. lemon juice   ½ cup oil
1 Tbs. mustard (optional)   2 cloves garlic (optional)

Mix lemon juice with mustard and minced garlic. Slowly add oil while stirring until oil is well blended.

Hazelnut Gravy

2 cups hazelnut milk   2 Tbs. tapioca flour
2 Tbs. oil   ¼ tsp. salt

Combine oil and milk. Stir in flour and slowly heat. Add any herb or spice that you like such as basil, thyme, dill, cayenne or black pepper. Simmer in sauce pan until thick.

DAY FOUR

Almond Gravy

2 cups almond milk   2 Tbs. chickpea flour
2 Tbs. oil   ¼ tsp. salt

Combine oil and milk. Stir in flour and slowly heat. Add any herb or spice that you like such as basil, thyme, dill, cayenne or black pepper. Simmer in sauce pan until thick.

NON-ROTATING RECIPES

These recipes use distilled white vinegar. Because it is a product of chemical wood decomposition it is unlikely to cause allergic reactions. It can be used on any day of the rotation.

Oil and Vinegar Dressing

3 Tbs. distilled white vinegar   2 garlic cloves (optional)
1 Tbs. mustard (optional)   ½ cup oil

Mix vinegar with mustard and minced garlic if tolerated. Slowly add oil while stirring until oil is well blended. Shake again before using. Use a herb vinegar for even better flavour.

Fresh Herb Vinegar

2 cups distilled white vinegar   2 Tbs. fresh herbs

Crush fresh herbs slightly and add to vinegar. Cover and let sit for one or two weeks. If too strong add more vinegar. Use tarragon, rosemary, thyme, savory, parsley, celery seed or a mixture of any of these.

Dried Herb Vinegar

2 cups distilled white vinegar   *2 tsp. dried herbs*

Crush dried herbs into vinegar. This can be used after one hour. Use tarragon, rosemary, thyme, savory, parsley, celery seed or a mixture of any of these.

Oil, Garlic and Lemon Juice Dressing

3 Tbs. lemon juice   *½ cup olive*
1 Tbs. mustard (optional)   *oil*
2 garlic cloves (optional)

Mix lemon juice with mustard and minced garlic if tolerated. Slowly add oil while stirring until oil is well blended.

Garlic Dill Dressing

½ lb. fresh tofu   *3 Tbs. lemon juice*
2 Tbs. oil   *1 tsp. garlic*
4 tsp. dill seed or ⅛ tsp. anise   *salt*

Blend all ingredients in blender; add a spoonful of water if necessary. Toss with salads or over fresh vegetables. Use in place of mayonnaise.

Sunflower Dressing (topping for potatoes)

1⅓ cups sunflower seeds   *1 Tbs. minced onion*
1 tsp. salt   *1⅔ cups water*
1 minced garlic clove   *⅓ cup lemon juice (to taste)*

Blend all ingredients. Excellent with avocado or tomato.

Noodles

Home Made Barley Noodles

2 eggs　　　　　　　　　　*1 cup barley flour*
1 Tbs. oil

In small food processor combine eggs and oil. Add flour and mix until a thick dough is formed. If it is too wet add more flour. Process with a pasta maker using more flour to prevent sticking and cook in rapidly boiling water for a couple of minutes until done.

Bean Noodles

Bean thread or bean starch noodles will become transparent when cooked. They can be used in place of wheat noodles in any recipe. They will be found in oriental grocery stores.

Mie Goreng (Indonesian Noodles)

¼ lb. bean starch/bean thread　　*2 Tbs. oil*
　　noodles　　　　　　　　　*¼ tsp. salt (optional)*
4 cups boiling water　　　　　*2-3 slices ginger root*
½ cup chopped peanuts or　　　*1 cup snow peas or peas*
　　cashews　　　　　　　　　*1 cup zucchini, sliced thinly*

Boil noodles briefly, about 5 minutes, until al dente and drain. Carefully roast nuts in a pan for 3-5 minutes or use roasted nuts. Saute ginger and vegetables until soft and add with noodles to nuts. Add salt or 2 Tbs. soy sauce (wheat free), if not yeast sensitive. You can use leftover or sauteed beef instead of nuts. Saute for 3 more minutes and serve hot. Serves 2. These noodles become translucent when cooked.

Spaghetti Squash

Pierce the squash with a fork in several places. Bake in a 350° oven until soft, about 45 to 60 minutes. Cut the squash in half. Scoop out the seeds in the centre. With a fork pull out the stringy squash pulp. Separate the strands, fluff them up and serve with a sauce. They taste and look like slightly crisp spaghetti.

DAY TWO

Corn Noodles

Corn noodles are available in natural food stores as macaroni or spaghetti. Do not overcook or they will become mushy. Serve with your usual sauces.

Macaroni with Quick Tomato Sauce

1½ cup corn macaroni
6 cups boiling water
1 large can plum
    tomatoes or
    5 large ripe tomatoes
⅛ tsp. cayenne (optional)
2 Tbs. oil

6 oz. tomato paste
½ onion, finely chopped
½ green pepper, finely
    chopped
¼ tsp. kelp, dulse or salt
    (optional)

Blend or strain the tomatoes. Saute other vegetables and add to tomatoes. Bring to boil and simmer about 10 minutes. Boil macaroni until softened. Do not overcook. It should be springy, not mushy. Pour sauce over noodles. Serves two. If you like, add ½ chopped chicken to the sauteeing vegetables. Spice up the sauce with any herbs you like such as oregano or basil.

DAY THREE

Rice Noodles

Rice noodles are available in a variety of forms. Those imported from China may be very thin or thick. In Thailand they are made flat. Often they are labelled as rice sticks. They should be cooked in boiling water until soft. The flat noodles will cook much faster. Serve with a sauce or instead of rice as a side dish. In Asia they are often served mixed with small pieces of sauteed vegetable, chicken or meat. These noodles can alternatively be served with your favourite pesto sauce (see recipe below).

Mie Goreng (Indonesian Noodles)

¼ lb. rice noodles
4 cups boiling water
½ cup filberts, chopped
2 Tbs. oil
¼ tsp. salt (optional)

2-4 slices ginger root, chopped
1 cup coarsely grated carrots
1 cup celery, sliced thinly
1 cup chopped spinach

Boil noodles in water until al dente, and drain. Carefully roast nuts in pan for 3-5 minutes or use roasted nuts. Saute ginger and vegetables until soft and add to noodles with nuts. Add salt. You can use leftover or sauteed carrot or shrimp instead of nuts. Saute for 3 more minutes and serve hot. Serves 2, or 1 very hungry person.

DAY FOUR

Home-made Oat Noodles

2 eggs
1 Tbs. oil

1 cup oat flour

In small food processor combine eggs and oil. Add flour and mix until a thick dough is formed. If it is too wet add more flour. Process with a pasta maker using more flour to prevent sticking and cook in rapidly boiling water for a couple of minutes until done.

Sweet Potato\Yam Noodles

These are also sometimes found in Japanese food stores. Check the label to be sure it does not have wheat flour added. They will become transparent when cooked.

Mie Goreng (Indonesian noodles)

¼ lb. 100% buckwheat or
   100% yam noodles
½ cup almonds, chopped
2 Tbs. oil

1 cup chopped broccoli or
   cauliflower
2-4 slices ginger root
1 cup finely sliced cabbage

Boil noodles until al dente and drain. Yam noodles become translucent. Roast nuts in pan carefully for 3-5 minutes or use roasted nuts. Steam broccoli until slightly soft. Then saute with cabbage and ginger until soft. Add salt if desired and add to noodles with nuts. Saute for 3 minutes and serve hot. You can saute pieces of any Day Four meats instead of nuts. Serves two.

Buckwheat Noodles

Buckwheat is not related to wheat and is usually well tolerated. However, most buckwheat noodles are made with wheat flour added. If the label lists flour, in addition to buckwheat flour then it contains wheat. It is possible to buy 100% buckwheat noodles in Japanese food stores. Often they are quite expensive. Cook them until softened but not overdone as they will crumble. In Japan they are often served cold, dipped in diluted soy sauce.

Home made Buckwheat Noodles

2 eggs
1 Tbs. oil

1¼ cup light buckwheat flour

In small food processor combine eggs and oil. Add flour and mix until a thick dough is formed. If it is too wet add more flour. Process with a pasta maker using more flour to prevent sticking and cook in rapidly boiling water for a couple of minutes until done.

Cannelloni

This basic recipe can be used in many different ways. Choose a crepe recipe from the Pancake section on page 87. Make ten four inch crepes and set aside.

1 Tbs. oil	*1 chopped celery stalk*
¼ lb. spinach or Swiss chard	*1 clove chopped garlic*
½ cup rice cake crumbs	*1 egg or alternative for binding*
½ lb. ground turkey, chicken,	*salt*
* beef or firm tofu*	*pepper*
1 chopped onion	*pinch of nutmeg*
½ chopped carrot	*tomato sauce (see page 154)*

Use a blender of food processor to make the rice cake crumbs. Wash the spinach or chard and while still damp place in a heavy pot. The washing water is enough to steam the vegetables. Steam for about three minutes until it is wilted. Then press out excess liquid and chop finely. Crumble tofu. Oil a pan and saute the meat or tofu on medium heat until almost done. In a separate pan saute the onion, garlic, carrot and celery. Omit any vegetables to which you react and add any other tolerated vegetables. Combine the meat or tofu, sauteed vegetables, chopped spinach, rice cake crumbs and egg. Add salt, pepper and nutmeg to taste. Place some of the stuffing in the centre of each crepe. Roll it into a tube and place in an oiled baking dish. Cover the cannelloni with pre-heated tomato sauce and bake in a pre-heated oven at 350° for about 20 minutes.

Cannelloni di Mare (Crab meat cannelloni)

Use the above recipe but substitute ½ lb. crab meat for the meat/tofu. Do not saute it but add it uncooked to the sauteed vegetables and spinach before stuffing the crepes.

Sauces for Noodles

DAY ONE

Zucchini Sauce

1 zucchini	*4 oz. artichoke hearts*
2 Tbs. oil	*2 anchovy fillets*

Slice the zucchini thinly and saute until soft in oil. Add the artichoke hearts and diced anchovy. Continue to saute until the anchovy starts to fall apart. Mix with cooked noodles and serve.

DAY TWO

Tomato Sauce

1 quart canned tomatoes	*2 Tbs. oil*
1 onion - diced (optional)	*½ tsp. basil*
2 cloves garlic diced (optional)	*½ tsp. oregano*
1 red or green pepper -diced	*black pepper to taste*

Bring the tomatoes to a boil in a large sauce pan. Saute the onion, garlic and pepper in oil until softened. Add to tomatoes and continue to cook on low heat until the sauce has become slightly thickened. Add basil, oregano and pepper and cook for 5 more minutes. This can be frozen, canned or used immediately.

DAY THREE

Parsley Sauce

1 cup parsley	*½ tsp. salt*
⅓ cup pine nuts	*⅓ cup oil*

Blend parsley, pine nuts, salt and oil until the mixture is smooth. For extra bite add a few capers or ¼ tsp. cayenne pepper. Mix with cooked noodles without cooking and serve.

Vegetable Sauce

1 carrot
1 stalk celery
3 water chestnuts

2 Tbs. parsley
2 Tbs. oil

Slice all of the vegetables into thin sections. Saute in the oil until quite soft. Add the parsley and cook for 2 more minutes. Mix with cooked noodles and serve.

DAY FOUR

Broccoli Sauce

1 stalk broccoli
½ cup cauliflower pieces
1 Tbs. grated ginger

2 Tbs. oil
1 tsp. oregano

Slice the broccoli and steam with the cauliflower. Saute ginger in the oil for 3 minutes and then add the vegetables and the oregano. Mix with cooked noodles and serve.

NON-ROTATING RECIPES

Pesto

2 cups fresh basil
½ cup parsley
½ cup olive oil

¼ cup pine nuts
1 clove garlic (optional)
½ tsp. salt

Place all of the ingredients in a blender of food processor and blend until smooth. Serve without cooking by mixing in a few tablespoons with noodles. It can be frozen and then used when needed.

Puddings

DAY ONE

Banana Fig Pudding

6 oz. tofu
½ small banana

1 Tbs. fig spread (see
    page 187)

Blend all of the ingredients together. Serve cool.

DAY TWO

Raspberry Pudding

¾ cup raspberry or grape juice
2 Tbs. corn starch or 3 Tbs.
    potato flour

3 egg yolks (optional)
2 cups broken raspberries

Make raspberry juice by defrosting frozen raspberries and pouring off
the juice or by lightly crushing fresh berries and letting them sit for a
few hours. Combine juice, cornstarch or potato flour in a pan. If using
potato flour, do not allow to boil or the pudding will thin and serve
soon after cooking. Cook for a few minutes over medium heat stirring
frequently until thickened. Reduce to low heat and add egg yolks if
used. Stir in berries and cook 5 minutes until thick and smooth.
Makes a tart pudding.

Millet Pudding

2 cups cooked millet
¼ cup raisins

1½ cups sesame milk (see
    page 68)

Mix millet, raisins and sesame milk in a deep casserole dish. Bake 20
minutes at 325°. Serve hot with additional sesame milk.

Berry Pudding

¾ cup berry or grape juice
1 Tbs. corn starch
1 Tbs. potato flour

3 egg yolks (optional)
2 cups sliced and mashed
  berries

Combine juice, cornstarch, and potato flour in a pan. Cook for 10 minutes over medium heat. Stir occasionally until thickened. Reduce to low heat and add egg yolks. Cook 5 minutes until thick and smooth. Remove from heat and stir in berries.

Raisin Pudding

⅓ cup walnuts or pecans
  (optional)

1 cup raisins
1 cup hot water

Wash raisins thoroughly. Soak in hot water until softened. Blend raisins, nuts, and water until smooth. Very sweet. Good as is or use as a topping on cereals or as a sugar alternative in recipes.

Millet Raisin Pudding

¾ cup millet
¼ tsp. salt
4 cups water or juice
½ cup raisins

2 Tbs. corn syrup (optional)
1 tsp. vanilla
½ cup sesame seeds or walnut
  pieces

Cook millet in water and salt until it boils. Add remaining ingredients and pour into a casserole dish. Cover and bake at 350° F. for 1 hour. Stir occasionally. Good served with berries. Can be flavoured with a pinch of cinnamon, ginger, cloves or cardamon. If you are not rotating, try with chopped dates and slices of raw apple in place of raisins.

Amaranth or Quinoa Pudding

2 cups cooked amaranth or
quinoa (see page 74)
1/4 cup chopped dates

1 1/2 cups hazelnut milk (see
page 70)

Mix amaranth or quinoa, dates and hazelnut milk in a deep casserole dish. Bake 20 minutes at 325°. Serve hot with additional hazelnut milk.

Fruit Pudding

1/3 cup rice flour
1/4 cup hazelnut butter or other
nut butter or seed meal

3 cups orange or other
fruit juice

In a saucepan, combine flour and fruit juice. Cook over medium heat for 10 minutes until thickened. Stir frequently. Add nut butter and puree in blender until creamy.

Brown Rice Pudding

2 cups cooked brown rice
1/4 cup chopped dates

1 1/2 cups hazelnut milk (see
page 70)

Mix all ingredients. Pour into deep casserole dish. Bake 20 minutes at 325° F. Serve hot with additional nut milk.

Fruit Juice Tapioca Pudding

The same as Non-Dairy Tapioca Pudding below but using fruit juice such as orange or grapefruit instead of nut or seed milk.

Non-Dairy Tapioca Pudding

2 cups nut or seed milk   maple syrup to taste (optional)
4 Tbs. tapioca   ¼ tsp. vanilla (optional)

Soak tapioca in nut or seed milk for 15 minutes. Heat to boiling point. Stir occasionally until mixture begins to thicken. Do not allow to burn. Cool. Add sliced fruit and coconut and serve warm.

DAY FOUR

Apple Oat Pudding

1 cup rolled oats   1 cup apple juice
1 cup water   ½ apple

Combine water and apple juice and bring to boil in a saucepan. Add oats and reduce heat to simmer. Chop apple into ½ inch pieces. When oats are halfway cooked, add apple pieces.

NON-ROTATING RECIPES

Carob Tofu Pudding-no cooking

2 Tbs. carob powder   1½ tsp. vanilla
20 oz. soft tofu   ½ tsp. cinnamon
2 Tbs. tahini (see page 187) ¼ cup honey
2-3 Tbs. lemon juice

Add ingredients to bowl or blender. Whip or blend until light and fluffy. Put in serving bowls and chill until set. (If you can wait that long!)

Banana Pineapple Pudding

1 banana	1 tsp. agar agar flakes
1 small can pineapple pieces	¼ cup water

Sprinkle a little water on the agar agar flakes and let sit five minutes. Puree banana and pineapple in blender. Heat water and stir in agar agar flakes until dissolved. Cool and add to fruit. Blend again and cool. Serve chilled.

Carob Pudding

1 Tbs. carob powder	1 Tbs. lemon juice
10 oz. soft tofu	½ tsp. vanilla extract
1 Tbs. hazelnut, peanut or sesame seed butter	¼ cup date jam

In a blender puree all of the ingredients until they are smooth and light. Pour into bowls and chill. Makes 2-4 servings.

Fruit and Oatmeal Pudding

½ cup chopped dried apple or currants	2 cups cooked oatmeal
½ cup seeds or chopped nuts (optional)	1 cup diced fruit
	⅓ cup juice

Combine and pour into well-oiled casserole dish. Bake at 375° F. for 15 minutes until hot.

Corn Pudding

2½ cups sesame or soy milk
  or apple juice
½ cup cornmeal
1 large egg, beaten lightly
  (optional)
2 apples
½ cup raisins

¼ cup unsulphured dark
  molasses
¼ tsp. ground ginger
¼ tsp. nutmeg
½ tsp. cinnamon
¼ tsp. salt

In a large saucepan stir cornmeal into milk or apple juice. Stir frequently and cook over medium heat until quite thick. Remove from heat and add egg if used. Chop apple into ¼-½ inch pieces. Stir in molasses, ginger, nutmeg, cinnamon, salt, apples, and raisins. Mix well. Turn into well oiled bread pan or casserole dish. Bake at 325° for 20 minutes. Serve hot or cold. Good for breakfast if made the night before or for dessert.

Pies & Cakes

DAY ONE

Banana Cheese Cake

2 lbs. soft tofu
½ cup oil

¼ cup pineapple juice
2 bananas

Slice one banana thinly and place the slices on an oiled 7 inch pie plate to form a base for the cheese cake. Combine all other ingredients in blender and blend until creamy. Pour filling onto banana slices and bake at 350° for 40 minutes or until top is golden brown and cheese cake has firmed. Serve chilled with fruit topping if desired.

Squash Pie

¼ cup tofu
2 cups squash
¼ soy milk

¼ cup fig puree
½ tsp. ginger & cinnamon
¼ tsp. cloves & cloves

This pie does not require a crust. Use acorn, hubbard or butternut squash. Cut into sections and remove stem. Steam till soft. When cool enough to handle peel and puree. Put all ingredients in blender and blend until combined. Pour into oiled pie plate. Bake at 425 ° for 15 minutes. This tastes and looks exactly like pumpkin pie.

Pecan Cake

½ cup raisin jam (see
    page 187)

2 cups shelled pecans
2 large eggs

Grind pecans into flour in a blender. Add raisin jam and mix thoroughly. Beat eggs until they are as light and frothy as possible. Slowly add the nut flour. Pour into an oiled 8x8 inch pan and bake at 350° for 35-40 minutes. Serve when cool. If not rotating try this with other nuts as well.

Upside Down Cake

2 cups sliced apple, peach,
    apricot or plum
⅓ cup oil
¼ cup date jam
¼ cup almond milk or water

1 tsp. vanilla extract
2½ tsp. baking powder
2⅓ cups oat flour
¼ cup arrowroot powder
⅔ cup almond milk or water

Place a single layer of the sliced fruit on the bottom of an oiled 10 inch pie plate. Blend the oil, date jam, ¼ cup of almond milk and vanilla extract until smooth. Mix the baking powder, oat flour and arrowroot powder. Add the blended mixture and the rest of the almond milk or water and stir until well combined. Pour over the fruit to form a smooth layer. Bake at 375° for about 25 minutes. Cover the pie plate with a plate and turn the pie plate over and ease the cake out onto the plate.

Fresh Strawberry Pie

¼ cup cold water
2 Tbs. corn starch

4 cups strawberries

Line a 9 inch pie plate with a crust from the list below. Mix the corn starch with water until the paste is smooth. Clean and slice the strawberries. Pour the corn starch mixture over the berries, gently stir and allow to sit for 15 minutes. Pour berries into pie crust. Sprinkle with a topping from the crust list below. Bake at 450° for ten minutes and then at 350° for 40 minutes. If using frozen berries follow instructions for Frozen Blueberry Pie.

DAY THREE

Frozen Blueberry Pie

3 cups partly defrosted frozen
   blueberries

3 Tbs. tapioca starch
2 Tbs. oil

Line a 9 inch pie plate with a crust chosen from the list below.
Combine all of the ingredients above in a bowl. Allow to sit for 15
minutes. Pour into the pie crust. Sprinkle with topping from crust list
below. Bake at 450° for 10 minutes and then at 350° for 50 minutes.
If using fresh blueberries follow instructions for Fresh Strawberry Pie.

DAY FOUR

Apple Peach Pie

2 cups sliced apples
2 cups fresh sliced peaches
½ tsp. cinnamon (optional)

⅛ tsp. nutmeg (optional)
3 Tbs. tapioca starch

Line a 9 inch pie plate with a crust chosen from the list below. Use
sweet cooking apples like Spy, Cortland or Rome. Steam the apple
slices until they are softened. Combine all of the ingredients and stir
gently until well mixed. Pour into pie crust and arrange in layers.
Cover with topping from crust list below. Bake at 400° for 35 minutes
and then 375° for 40 minutes.

NON-ROTATING RECIPES

Hazelnut Cake

2 cups shelled hazelnuts
2 large eggs

½ cup maple syrup or raisin
   pudding

Grind hazelnuts into a flour in a blender. Mix with raisin pudding or maple syrup. Beat eggs until light and frothy. Gently mix with hazelnuts. Pour into a greased 8 inch pan and bake at 350° F. for 35-40 minutes. Allow to cool before serving.

Citrus Rice Cake

This cake is very much like a cheesecake in texture and consistency.

1 cup Italian Arborio rice	½ tsp. vanilla extract
1 litre soy, rice or nut milk	3 large eggs
⅛ tsp. salt	grated yellow peel of 1 lemon
½ cup date jam (see	or orange
page 188)	3 Tbs. lemon or orange juice

Heat the soy milk until almost boiling and add the rice. Stir frequently so that the rice does not stick. Cook until all the soy milk is absorbed and then let cool. Combine the eggs and date jam. With an electric mixer whisk for two minutes. Add grated lemon peel and juice and mix again. Add the cooked rice and again mix well. Oil a spring form cake pan. Pour the mixture into the pan and bake at 325° for about 30 minutes until it is firm in the centre.

Date Oatmeal Cake

½ cup oat flour	2 cups rolled oats
1 tsp. cinnamon	½ cup oil
1 tsp. cloves	2 eggs or alternative for binding
1 tsp. baking powder	1 cup coarsely chopped walnuts
1 cup boiling water	1½ cups finely chopped dates

Sift together into a bowl the flour, cinnamon, cloves and baking powder. Pour 1 cup boiling water over 2 cups rolled oats, mix well, cool slightly, then blend in the oil, eggs, walnuts and dates. Pour oatmeal mixture into dry ingredients and mix well. Bake in an 8 inch square pan at 350° F. for 45 minutes or until done.

Millet Apple Cake

⅓ cup vegetable shortening
2 eggs
¼ cup sweetener
1 tsp. vanilla
½ tsp. nutmeg
¼ tsp. cinnamon
1½ cups millet flour

¼ cup rice flour
3 tsp. baking powder
½ salt
½ cup chopped nuts
½ cup chopped raisins
1 cup apple juice

Cream shortening, eggs, sweetener, and vanilla. Combine these with dry ingredients and gradually add apple juice. Beat until smooth. Pour into oiled 9 inch cake pan and bake at 375° F. for 25-30 minutes or until done.

Carob Nut Log

½ cup carob powder
½ cup ground mixed nuts
½ cup sesame seeds
½ cup pecans or large walnut pieces
¼ cup honey

2 Tbs. unrefined oil
½ cup unhulled sunflower seeds
½ cup soy or other flour
½ cup water if needed

Combine all ingredients and mix thoroughly. Refrigerate. When it is fully chilled, oil your hands and shape the mixture into a log or roll into small balls. Roll the log in additional finely chopped seeds or nuts until well coated. Store, covered, in refrigerator. Slice to serve. The flavour is best after a few days' refrigeration. The log will keep for weeks.

Tofu Cheesecake

Filling:

2 lbs. soft tofu	2 tsp. vanilla
¼ cup pineapple juice	1 banana
½ cup oil	

Crust:

2 cups coconut, or 1½ cups coconut and ½ cup ground roasted or raw nuts and seeds

Mix crust ingredients together and press into large pie plate. Combine all filling ingredients in blender and blend until creamy (2 batches might be easier). Pour filling into crust and bake at 350° F. for 40 minutes or until top is golden brown and cake has jelled. Serve chilled with fruit if desired. A full recipe will fit into a pie plate with 7 inch bottom.

Banana Pie

½ cup dates	½ cup coconut
½ cup seeds or filberts	4 bananas
2½ cups water	1 tsp. vanilla
½ cup arrowroot powder	

Liquify nuts and dates in blender with water. Slowly while stirring, add liquid to arrowroot. Heat and stir until it thickens. Mash 2 bananas and add along with vanilla. Slice 2 bananas into bottom of pie dish, sprinkle coconut over bananas, cover with filling and chill.

Strawberry Torte

2 Tbs. honey	½ cup tofu
1 cup whole strawberries	8 oz. can crushed pineapple
pinch of nutmeg	

Crush strawberries. Whip tofu and add all other ingredients. Mix until smooth. Refrigerate till chilled. garnish with nutmeg and serve.

Peach Cream Pie

2½ cups sliced peaches or
   other fruit
1 tsp. oil
1 Tbs. sweetener (eg. raisin jam)
1 cup water

¼ cup sesame butter or
   ground nuts
2 Tbs. arrowroot powder
coconut

Heat oil and saute peaches. Mix sweetener, sesame butter or ground nuts and water. Raise to a boil and add arrowroot. Cook 3 minutes. Add peaches. Sprinkle a thick layer of coconut onto pie plate. Pour in filling and chill.

Pumpkin Pie

2 eggs or ¼ cup tofu
2 cups pumpkin puree
¾ cups soy milk
2 Tbs. molasses
2 Tbs. honey

coconut or ground nuts
½ tsp. ginger
¼ tsp. cloves
¾ tsp. nutmeg
½ tsp. cinnamon

Sprinkle a thick layer coconut or nuts onto pie plate. Put all ingredients in blender and blend until combined. Pour onto coconut pie crust and bake at 425° F. for 15 minutes.

Strawberry Flan

1 tsp. vanilla
¼ cup tapioca flour
1¼ cups soy milk

3 eggs
2 Tbs. honey or sweetener
coconut or ground nuts

Sprinkle a thick layer coconut or nuts onto pie plate. Beat the eggs, honey, tapioca and vanilla together. Scald the soy milk and add to egg mixture. Stir and cook in a double boiler over rapidly boiling water for 12 minutes stirring to prevent lumps. Tapioca will thicken as it cools. Pour onto coconut pie crust, cool and top with sliced strawberries.

Crusts

Seed Crust and Topping

1 cup pumpkin or sunflower seeds

In blender, blend seeds until a smooth powder is formed. Press into pie shell or sprinkle on pie filling pressing slightly.

DAY TWO

Polenta Crust

½ cup cornmeal   2 cups water

Add cornmeal to water and bring to boil while stirring. Cook 15 minutes of longer. Lower heat and stir frequently until the cornmeal has firmed. If too thick add more water. You may want to add ¼ tsp. salt or vanilla extract. When firm enough to keep shape pour thin layer into pie plate and shape along sides. Add ¼ cup raisin jam (see page 187) if you are using this for a fruit pie.

Cooked Millet Crust

½ cup millet   ½ cup water

Cook millet until water is absorbed. It should be slightly sticky. If not add a little more water and cook longer. Pour into pie plate and press into thin layer. When adding fruit to this be sure that it covers the edges of the crust. The crust will dry out where it is exposed. If you like, add ½ cup ground sesame seeds to the millet.

Sesame Pecan Topping

½ cup sesame seeds   ½ cup pecans

In a blender, blend the ingredients until they form a smooth flour. Sprinkle on top of the filling and pat into place.

DAY THREE

Coconut Crust

2 cups coconut or 1½ cups coconut and ½ cup ground hazelnuts

Use fresh coconut or roast it carefully in a pan over medium heat until it stars to brown. Mix crust ingredients and press into an oiled pie plate.

Hazelnut Topping

1 cup hazelnuts

In blender, blend hazelnuts until a smooth powder is formed. Sprinkle on pie filling pressing slightly.

Rice Flour Pie Crust

Mix in a bowl:
2 cups rice flour or flakes   ½ tsp. cinnamon
½ cup vegetable shortening

Pat mixture evenly in a 9" square pan. Bake 10 minutes in a hot oven.

Crunchy Oat Crust and Topping

2 cups raw rolled oats
5 Tbs. oil
3 Tbs. prune spread (see
    page 189)

½ tsp. cinnamon
½ cup chopped almonds
¼ cup oat flour

Combine all ingredients and mix well. Apply evenly over top of pie pressing into place.

Oat Pizza or Pie Crust

1½ cup oat flour
1 tsp. baking soda

2 Tbs. oil
½ cup water

Combine flour and baking soda. Add oil and water. Press into oiled pie plate. If dough sticks to fingers sprinkle a little flour onto the dough. Add fillings. Makes enough for two pies. This is difficult to place on top of a pie.

Cookies

If your cookies are too hard and dry you may need to add more oil or use flour that is ground finer. If they are undercooked, the batter may be too moist or they may need more baking.

DAY ONE

Banana Cookies

4 figs
1 cup chickpea flour
1 tsp. baking powder

1 medium banana
¼ cup oil

Soak the figs in boiling water and leave overnight. Combine the chickpea flour and baking powder. Blend the soaked figs, banana and oil until smooth. Add to the flour and mix thoroughly. Spoon onto a greased cookie sheet. Press down with a wet fork and bake at 350° for 15 minutes.

Peanut/Cashew Butter Cookies

1 cup peanut or cashew butter
¼ cup oil
½ tsp. vanilla (optional)
½ cup honey or fig spread
 (see page 187)

1 Tbs. psyllium husk soaked in
 3 Tbs. water
¼ tsp. salt
½ tsp. baking powder
1½ cups chickpea flour

Preheat oven to 350° F. Mix liquid ingredients together until smooth. Add the flour. Mix well. Form into small balls with hands, place on oiled cookie sheet and flatten each with a fork. Bake about 10 minutes. Be careful as they burn easily.

DAY TWO

Corn Cookies

½ cup corn flour
½ cup corn meal
1 tsp. baking powder
¼ cup raisins

¼ cup water
1 egg
2 Tbs. oil

Mix together the corn flour, corn meal and baking powder, In a blender, puree the raisins, water, egg and oil. Add these to the flour mixture. Combine well and drop spoonfuls onto an oiled cookie sheet. Bake at 350° for 15 minutes. Makes one dozen.

DAY THREE

Biscotti al Riso

1 cup brown rice flour
1 Tbs. tapioca flour
1 tsp. baking powder
1 egg well beaten
¼ cup sugar or sweetener

⅓ cup oil
⅓ tsp. anise extract
¼ cup chopped roasted
    hazelnuts

Combine flours and baking powder. Beat egg until light and add oil, anise extract and sweetener. Add dry ingredients and then nuts. Shape into a roll about 2 inches in width. Flatten to ½ inch. Bake on a cookie sheet at 375° for 25 minutes until light golden. Watch the bottom edge for early browning. Allow to cool for 5 minutes and slice into ½ inch segments. Store in an airtight container. If you are rotating your foods skip eggs on the previous and next rotation.

Rice Crispy Squares

½ cup hazelnut butter
½ cup date jam(see page 188)

3 Tbs. oil
3 cups puffed rice

Blend the nut butter, date jam and oil together. Mix in the puffed rice until it is well coated. Pour into a 9x9 inch pan. Refrigerate and serve cold cut into one inch squares. This makes a soft chewy square. If you use crispy puffed rice, the result will be crispier and lighter.

Rice-flake Cookies

½ cup date jam(see page 188) ¼ cup sweet rice flour
⅔ cup orange juice 1 cup rolled rice flakes
1 tsp. vanilla extract (optional) 1 tsp. cinnamon (optional)
⅓ cup oil ¼ cup coconut (optional)
¾ cup rice flour

Preheat oven to 350°. Blend dates with oil and vanilla extract if used. Pour ⅓ cup of orange juice over rice flakes and let sit for 10 minutes. Mix rice flours, rice flakes and cinnamon. Add blended mixture and remaining orange juice. Stir in coconut if used. Oil a cookie sheet and drop cookies onto sheet. Press each cookie down with a fork. Bake 15 to 20 minutes. Makes 20.

Coconut Rice Cookies

1 cup rice flour ¼ cup orange juice or water
1½ tsp. baking powder ½ cup coconut
4 Tbs. oil ½ cup ground hazelnuts
¼ cup date jam   (optional)
1 tsp. vanilla extract (optional)

Combine flour and baking powder and stir oil in. Combine date jam, vanilla extract and water or juice. Combine coconut and ground nuts. Alternately add portions of the nut and water mixtures to the flour until all are well mixed. Shape into a roll, wrap in wax paper and chill until firm. Slice the roll in ¼ inch widths and place on an oiled cookie sheet. Bake at 350° for 10 minutes or until browned.

DAY FOUR

Scotch Biscotti

3½ cups oat flour
¼ cup tapioca flour
3 tsp. baking powder
3 eggs well beaten
⅔ cup sugar or sweetener

½ cup oil
1 tsp. almond extract
¾ cup chopped roasted
   almonds

Combine flours and baking powder. Beat eggs until light and add oil, almond extract and sweetener. Add dry ingredients and then nuts. Shape into 3 rolls about 2 inches in width. Flatten to ½ inch. Bake at 375° for 25-30 minutes until light golden. Allow to cool for 5 minutes and slice into ½ inch segments. Store in an airtight container when cool. If you are rotating your foods skip eggs and tapioca on the previous and next rotation.

Oatmeal Cookies

½ cup dried apples - diced
½ apple - grated
⅓ cup apple juice
1 tsp. vanilla extract (optional)
½ cup oil
¼ cup arrowroot

¾ cup oat flour
1 cup rolled oats
½ tsp. baking powder
1 tsp. cinnamon (optional)
¼ cup roasted chopped
   almonds (optional)

Preheat oven to 350°. Mix dried apples, grated apple, apple juice, vanilla extract if used and oil together. Mix arrowroot, oat flour, rolled oats, cinnamon and baking powder. Add wet ingredients. Stir in almonds if used. Oil a cookie sheet and drop cookies onto sheet. Press each cookie down with a fork. Bake 15 to 20 minutes. Makes 18. These cookies will be very crumbly. To make them more firm if you are not rotating add one beaten egg or ¼ cup well blended tofu.

Ice Cream and Ices

Some of the recipes call for an ice cream maker. The newest type has an inner container that is frozen prior to use. It contains a gel that retains the cold for a prolonged period and freezes the ice cream. Follow the manufacturers recommendations for making the ice cream after you have put the mix in the container for freezing.

Use soft tofu in these recipes if you can find it. Other tofus will have a stronger soy flavour. It is available in oriental and natural food stores. To make any of these recipes different add coconut, chopped nuts, diced dry fruit or any pureed or whole fruit pieces when the ice cream is just starting to freeze. You could also use these to top the ice cream.

Freeze any juice in a mould and insert sticks to make a delicious frozen treat for hot days.

DAY ONE

Fruit Ice Cream

1½ cups pineapple juice
1 tsp. slippery elm powder
juice of ½ lemon or ¼ cup
   extra pineapple juice

¼ cup honey (optional)
1 cup cashews
2 Tbs. oil

Blend above ingredients until smooth. Add diced fruit if you like, such as 1 cup of figs (soaked), mango, banana or pineapple. Pour into a flat pan and freeze. Serve before it gets too hard. Children love this.

Carob Ice Cream

10 oz. soft tofu
½ tsp. vanilla extract
¼ cup unsweetened carob
   chips (optional)

¼ cup carob powder
¼ cup fig spread (see
   page 187 - optional)

Blend all ingredients together except carob chips and place in an ice cream maker. Add carob chips halfway through freezing process.

Vanilla Ice Cream

1 Tbs. agar agar flakes	1 Tbs. vanilla
1 cup water	2 cups water
1 cup cashews	⅓ cup oil
¼ cup honey	

Soak agar agar flakes in water. Boil one minute and then cool for one minute. Add cashews, vanilla and water. Blend all the ingredients except oil. Add oil slowly while blending. Freeze in a bowl or flat dish.

Pineapple Ice Cream

¾ cup crushed pineapple	1 egg white beaten till foamy
½ cup pineapple juice	(optional if rotating)
½ cup other fruit juice	

Add pineapple and juices to beaten egg white. If rotating, juice a melon or mango or soak 4 dried figs in water overnight and use ½ cup of the resulting liquid. Place in ice cream maker. Follow machine directions for making ice cream.

DAY THREE

Hazelnut Coconut Ice Cream

3 cups hot water	⅓ cup rice syrup or sweetener
1 cup coconut	⅓ cup safflower oil
1 tsp. slippery elm	1 Tbs. vanilla.
½ cup hazelnuts	

Blend hot water, coconut, slippery elm and hazelnuts and then strain. Add rice syrup, oil and vanilla and blend again. Freeze and blend once more. Freeze a second time. It should be served before it is solidly frozen. For carob-coconut just add 3 Tbs. carob powder. You could also blend the ingredients and freeze them in an ice cream maker.

Orange Coconut Sherbet

1 Tbs. agar agar flakes

1 cup water

1 tsp. lemon juice

1 cup orange juice

½ cup coconut

1 tsp. slippery elm

¼ cup rice syrup or sweetener (to taste)

¼ cup oil

2 cups fresh fruit (oranges, tangerines, dates)

Dissolve agar agar flakes in water. Soak for 1 minute, then boil 1 minute, and cool 1 minute. Blend juice and coconut. Add agar agar and remaining ingredients. Blend until smooth. Put in freezer. Serve before it gets too hard. The agar agar does not fit in this rotation day. But it can be used if not used in the previous rotation.

DAY FOUR

Peach Ice

Blend canned or cooked peaches until smooth. Pour into a mould and insert sticks. Eat when frozen.

NON-ROTATING RECIPES

Peach Ice Cream

10 oz. soft tofu

¼ cup fruit juice eg. apple juice

8 oz. peaches

Blend all the ingredients thoroughly and place in ice cream maker. Follow your specific machine's directions for making ice cream.

Coconut Pineapple Ice Cream

1 cup coconut milk (canned
  or see page 70)

1 cup crushed pineapple
¼ cup date jam

In a blender whip all of the ingredients together. Place in your ice cream maker. Follow your specific machine's directions for making ice cream.

Berry Ice Cream

10 oz. soft tofu
¼ cup fruit juice or sweetener
  (optional)

10 oz. raspberries, blueberries,
  or strawberries etc.

Blend all the ingredients thoroughly and place in ice cream maker. Follow your specific machine's directions for making ice cream.

Desserts

Tofu Yogurt

8 oz. soft tofu

½ tsp. vanilla extract

¼ tsp. ascorbic acid powder

2 Tbs. fig spread (see page 187)

fruit (see instructions)

Blend the tofu, vanilla extract, ascorbic acid and fig spread together until smooth. Add any fruit that you wish to use. Pineapple, banana and mango fit the rotation.

Frozen Banana

Frozen banana is delicious. Peel, cut into chunks and freeze. Pour on 1-2 Tbs. of pineapple, lemon or lime juice (optional) and serve. Alternatively, blend the semi-frozen chunks and serve, or re-freeze for later use.

Carob Chip Cookies

½ cup sweetener (eg. fig spread)

½ cup oil

½ cup tofu or 2 eggs

1 tsp. vanilla

½ cup soy flour

¾ cup chickpea flour

2 tsp. baking powder

½-1 cup carob chips

Combine sweetener, oil, egg and vanilla in a bowl and add the remaining ingredients. Form into 1½ inch flat cookies. Bake at 375° F. for 8-10 minutes. If using eggs skip them in the next rotation.

Fried Banana

Peel a not overly ripe banana. Slice in half lengthwise. Fry in 4 Tbs. oil. Serve with 1-2 Tbs. of pineapple, lemon or lime juice (optional). It will become very soft and sweet.

DAY TWO

Strawberry Crisp

4 cups fresh sliced strawberries
2 Tbs. cornstarch

¼ cup corn syrup (to taste, optional)

Simmer strawberries until cooked. Add cornstarch and syrup and simmer until it begins to thicken. Place in bowl and cover with topping of ground walnuts, pecans and sesame seeds or make a lower crust of ground nuts, and seeds with a little oil and add strawberry filling. Bake in oven at 350° for 15 minutes.

Berry Agar Agar Mould

2 Tbs. agar agar flakes
1 cup cold water
1 cup hot water

1 cup berry juice
¼ cup corn syrup or sweetener

Mix agar agar flakes with cold water and let sit for 1 minute. Add hot water. Boil 2 minutes, let cool and add juice and sweetener. Cover bottom of glass mould with berries. Pour part of jelly over fruit and allow to set. Repeat to form layers of fruit and jelly.

Puffed Millet Squares

½ cup tahini (see page 187)
½ cup raisin pudding (see page 157)

3 Tbs. oil
3 cups puffed millet

In a blender combine sesame butter, raisin pudding and oil. Blend until smooth. Stir into puffed millet until well combined. KPour into a square cake pan. Chill and serve.

Millet Squares

1 cup washed millet
3½ cups water or soy milk
2 Tbs. oil

cinnamon
chopped fruit

Bring water or soy milk to a boil. Add washed millet and a dash of salt and simmer for 35 45 minutes. Add oil and cool. Then spread mixture on cookie sheet and sprinkle with sweetener or chopped fruit and cinnamon. Bake for 20 minutes in a hot oven. Serve with apple sauce or stewed fruit

DAY THREE

Coconut Dates

Slice soft pitted dates open. Stuff with finely cut coconut. Wonderful to pop in your mouth.

Blueberry Crisp

4 cups blueberries

1-2 cups filberts or pine nuts or crumbled rice cakes

Place thawed or fresh blueberries into casserole dish. Grind nuts or rice cakesin blender and sprinkle on berries. Bake at 400° F. for about 15 minutes.

Coconut Orange Dates

¾ cup nut or seed milk
7-9 dates

¼ tsp. orange or lemon rind
2 Tbs. coconut

Blend all ingredients until smooth. Pour over cooked rice and serve as is or after warming carefully on low heat.

Pear Crumble

28 oz. canned pears or 2 lb. raw
   pears peeled -simmered for 10
   minutes in ½ cup water
1 tsp. vanilla

2 Tbs. light oil
1 Tbs. maple syrup (optional)
½ cup sliced almonds

Drain canned pears and cut into ¼ inch slices (save juice). Layer the pears in an 8x8 inch pan. Combine juice of pears, vanilla and maple syrup. Drizzle over pears. Sprinkle with almonds. Drizzle oil over almonds. Bake at 350° F. for 10 minutes.

Nut-Apricot Cobbler

Soak unsulphured dried apricots in water or juice until soft. Puree in blender. Serve in sherbet cups. Sprinkle with finely chopped almonds or Brazil nuts.

Apple Rhubarb Crisp

Place 2-3 cups of stewed apples or pears and/or rhubarb in a casserole dish. Cover with either of the toppings below and bake for 20-30 minutes at 375° F. If you are not rotating fruit, try using blueberries or strawberries.

Topping 1: Combine
   2 cups oats
   ½ cup oat flour
   ⅓ cup maple syrup (optional)
   ¾ tsp. cinnamon or coriander

⅓ cup chopped almonds
   (optional)
¼ cup water or juice
¼ cup oil

Topping 2: Combine
   ½ cup light buckwheat flour
   ½ cup arrowroot flour
   2 Tbs. maple syrup (optional)
   ¾ tsp. cinnamon or cloves

⅓ cup chopped almonds
   (optional)
¼ cup oil

Rhubarb Sauce

1 cup finely diced rhubarb   ¼ cup maple syrup or prune
½ cup water or juice   spread (see page 189)

Place all ingredients in an electric blender and blend until smooth.
Serve in stemmed glasses at room temperature, chilled or heated.
Rhubarb is quite tart without a sweetener. Makes 2 servings.

Applesauce

Peel and slice 6 apples into a pot. Add ½ to 1 cup water. Cook
lightly for 5 minutes. Eat as is or place in blender and blend until
smooth. Add ¼ tsp. cinnamon if you like.

NON-ROTATING RECIPES

Soy Milk Custard

You could use your favourite custard recipe substituting soy milk for
cow's milk and add a bit more vanilla extract or use this recipe. If
you have a favourite custard powder, check the ingredients for
allergens.

2 cups soy milk   3 eggs-beaten
¼ cup fig spread   1 teaspoon vanilla extract

Combine the soy milk, fig spread and beat in the eggs. Add the vanilla
extract and pour into six custard cups. Place the cups in a pan of water
and bake at 325° for an hour or until done. Serve chilled.

Puffed Grain Squares

½ cup nut butter (peanut,
    sesame, etc.)
¼ cup honey
3 cups puffed rice, millet or
    corn

¼ cup vegetable shortening
½ cup carob chips (check
    ingredients) or ⅓ cup carob
    powder

Melt nut butter, shortening, honey and carob together. Mix in the puffed grain. Stir well until grain is coated. Place in 6x6 inch pan. Refrigerate.

Brownies

If you have an irresistible urge for chocolate and are not reactive to it, you can use this recipe with chocolate. Most contains milk. It is equally as good with carob. Use sugarless unsweetened chocolate.

1 cup flour - oat or light
    buckwheat (see page 62)
1 tsp. baking powder
2 oz. unsweetened chocolate
    or ½ cup carob powder
½ cup soft tofu

½ tsp. vanilla extract
2 cups date jam (see
    page 188)
⅔ cup oil
⅓ cup coarsely chopped
    walnuts

Mix the flour and baking powder together. Gently heat the oil and dissolve the chocolate or carob in it. Blend together the tofu, vanilla extract, date jam and oil/chocolate mix. Add to the flour and stir. Add walnuts if used. Bake in a 9x9 inch well oiled pan at 350° for 40-50 minutes. Baking time will depend on the wetness of the date jam. Serve when cool.

Strawberry Shortcake

2 pints strawberries
½ tsp. vanilla extract
2 cups oat flour
1 Tbs. baking powder
½ tsp. salt

3 Tbs. date jam (see
  page 188)
⅓ cup oil
⅔ cup apple juice or water

Cut the strawberries in half and add vanilla. Cook slowly until softened and juice forms. Mix oat flour, baking powder and salt. Mix date jam, oil and juice. Add to flour. Drop into 8 mounds on a cookie sheet letting them touch to make a 8 inch ring. Bake at 425° for 20-25 minutes. Cut cakes in half and spoon on strawberries then recap the cakes.

Fruit and Nut Crumble

4 portions stewed fruit (½ to 1
  cup per person) e.g. apples,
  blueberries, pears, apricots,
  berries, dates, peaches,
  separately or combined.

4 Tbs. honey
1 cup chopped nuts or seeds
2 Tbs. oil
4 Tbs. water

Mix oil, honey, water, and nuts. Spread half in the bottom of a casserole dish. Add fruit and top with remaining mixture. Bake at 400° F. for about 15 minutes.

Peanut Butter Squares

¼ cup honey
¼ cup peanut butter
½ tsp. salt
12 oz. tofu

2 tsp. vanilla
2 eggs
⅓ cup honey
⅓ cup carob powder

Blend honey, peanut butter, salt, tofu, vanilla and eggs and spread a flat layer in an 8x8 inch pan. Stir honey and carob together and pour onto of first layer. Marblize the layers with a knife. Freeze and enjoy.

Fruit Sauces, Jams and Spreads

DAY ONE

Fig Spread

8 oz. dried figs   water

Cover the figs with water and soak or simmer the figs until they are quite soft. Blend into a smooth puree. Use for a sweet spread or as a sweetener in recipes.

DAY TWO

Tahini (Sesame Seed Butter)

Tahini is made from ground sesame seeds. It can be used as a spread to replace peanut butter or as a base for sauces.

Raisin Jam/Puree

1 cup raisins   1 cup hot water

Wash raisins and soak in hot water until soft. Blend raisins with soaking water until quite smooth. This is very sweet. It can be used as a spread or as a sweetener in recipes.

Raspberry Sauce

½ cup raisins   ½ cup hot water
⅓ cup walnuts or pecans   ½ cup raspberries
  (optional)

Wash raisins thoroughly. Soak in hot water until softened. Blend raisins, nuts, raspberries and water until smooth. It has a sweet and tart flavour. It is good eaten as a pudding or use it to top cereals, muffins, pancakes or waffles.

DAY THREE

Date Jam

2-½ cups chopped dates
1-½ cups hot water

2 tsp. orange or lemon rind
(optional)

Chop dates into small pieces. Either soak dates in hot water until soft or cook over medium heat. If cooking, take care that they do not burn and stir frequently. If the dates are very dry you may need to add more water. Blend to make smoother.

Date Nut Jam

Add 1 cup of finely chopped filberts or hazelnuts to above recipe.

DAY FOUR

Prune Spread #1

2 cups pitted prunes
2 cups apple juice

½ tsp. cinnamon or
⅛ tsp. cloves

Simmer all ingredients in saucepan, stirring occasionally until prunes are tender and most of juice is gone. Puree when cool. Refrigerate in glass jars. Good as spread or as a filling for cookies.

Apricot Puree

Wash, slice and remove stone from apricots. Puree in a blender until smooth. Add a little water to a heavy pot and cook until slightly thick. Freeze or preserve in jars.

Prune Spread #2

8 oz. prunes   water

Cover the prunes with water and soak or simmer until they are soft.
Blend into a smooth puree. Use for a sweet spread or as a sweetener
in recipes.

Fruit Jam

½ cup dried apricots, peach or   ¼ cup almonds
   apple   1¼ cups apple juice
½ cup currants (or double one   ½ cup prunes
   of above fruits)

Combine the dried fruit and juice. Soak overnight. Add to blender ½
at a time and puree till smooth.

Tapenade

½ lb. pitted black cured olives   1 tsp. capers (optional)
3 anchovy fillets (optional)   2 Tbs. olive oil

Blend all of the ingredients in a food processor until smooth. It is a
wonderful salty spread or accompaniment to meats or vegetables. Try
with potatoes if not rotating.

Snacks

DAY ONE

Beverages

Chamomile Tea. Pineapple Juice

Nibbles

Peanuts, sunflower seeds, cashews, pistachios, figs, bananas, cucumber Peanut/Cashew Butter Cookies, Poppy Banana Bread, Tofu Yogurt.

Papadums

These are thin and crisp like large potato chips made from lentil flour and are available in East Indian food stores. They should be heated carefully in an oven and will become crisp like a chip.

DAY TWO

Beverages

Mint tea, grape juice, papaya juice, tomato juice

Nibbles

Walnuts, pecans, grapes, berries, dried papaya, corn bread, popcorn, corn chips, Raisin Pudding.

Corn Chips

Slice frozen (thawed) or fresh, soft corn tortillas into 6-8 wedges. Bake at 350° F. till crisp. These are low-fat, low-salt crispy corn chips.

Fruit and Nuts

Slice papaya into a bowl and add berries or grapes and top with walnuts or sesame seed milk (see milk alternatives).

DAY THREE

Beverages

Wintergreen tea. Orange, grapefruit, tangerine juice

Nibbles

Filberts, dates, orange, tangerine, rice cakes, rice crackers, carrot sticks, celery sticks, Carrot Bread, Amaranth Muffin.

DAY FOUR

Beverages

Ginger tea, rose hip tea. Apple juice.

Nibbles

Almonds, Brazil nuts, roasted chestnuts, dried or fresh apples, pears - dried or fresh, prunes, peaches, cherries, oat cakes.

Canning and Freezing

If you want to enjoy organically grown or seasonal fruit all year round then freezing and canning are essential. You will have on hand a variety of tolerated fruits that might be otherwise unobtainable. Canning retards spoilage by destroying micro-organisms on the fruit and denaturing enzymes that spoil the fruit. It must be done carefully if the fruit is to be useable for the whole year. Acid fruits are easy to can and quite safe. Non-acid fruits and vegetables require more care and specialty books should be consulted. You can preserve a years' supply of a fruit in an evening if you are organized. It can become a family event. Watch for organically grown produce in the markets.

Bulk fruit is often obtainable directly from the grower, at farmer's markets or from stores. Each fruit has its own season and you will soon be accustomed to the progression of berries, cherries, apricots, peaches, blueberries, pears, apples and tomatoes through the summer. Buying at the peak of the season, you will find prices the lowest.

Canning works out best with firmer fruit such as cherries, peaches, pears, apples or tomatoes. The easiest method of canning is in a boiling water bath.

You will need:
1. *a large canner pot with a rack for jars and a top for the pot*
2. *canning jars that will fit into your canner*
3. *self sealing lids and rings for the jars*
4. *syrup for the fruit*
5. *fruit*
6. *ladles, tongs, 2 or 3 pots of various sizes*

First check that the jars are very clean, not cracked or chipped and that you have enough of the right sized rings and lids. Add enough water to the canner and bring to boiling. Remember not to fill it to the top since the jars will displace a lot of the water.

Syrup

The purpose of the syrup is to transmit the heat of the water bath to the fruit and to maintain the texture and flavour of the fruit. Most books recommend excessive amounts of sugar in the syrup. Instead you could use fruit juice. Use apple, white grape, pineapple or citrus. Choose a juice whose flavour will enhance, blend with or be hidden by the fruit. You could even make your own juice by cooking down some of the fruit in advance. Peaches and tomatoes do this very nicely. Use between ¼ and ⅓ cup of juice in each cup of liquid. About 1 cup of syrup will be needed for each quart jar. Have the syrup close to boiling just before adding to jars.

Fruit

Choose fruit that is unblemished and not mouldy or spoiled. Wash or peel. Remove stems and seeds. Cherries may be pitted or left with pits in. Some people will blanch the whole fruit by dipping in boiling water for 5 minutes. We seldom bother. Dipping peaches in hot water for a minute makes them easier to peel. Cut larger fruit into useable sections. If the fruit will be sitting for some time before canning, sprinkle with a little ascorbic acid (Vitamin C) powder. This will slow down discolouration. You may want to pack fruit sauces such as apple, apricot or plum sauce. Clean and cut up the fruit and cook slowly until thickened. If you cook long enough, they will form a thick buttery or jam-like spread.

Pack jars with fruit firmly but do not crush. Leave about ½ inch of space at the top of jars. Pour in syrup. A ladle and large funnel makes this less messy. If necessary prod fruit with a knife to release air pockets. Wipe top of jar and add lids. Screw on rings. Check the manufacturers instructions on the box of lids. Different brands require different pretreatment. If you do not follow instructions, the lids may not seal. Place in the boiling water of canner and be sure the jars are covered by 1 inch of water. Replace water if it boils away.

Count time of processing from when water comes to boil again after adding jars.

Remove from canner after cooking and allow to cool. You should hear the lids snap or see that they have become depressed as the jars seal. If the lids are popped up you should check the manufacturers instructions on how to process the lids and redo the jar.

Canning times

Applesauce, rhubarb: 10 min.   Apricots, plums: 25 min.
Apples, berries, cherries: 15 min.   Tomatoes: 45 min.
Grapes, peaches, pears: 25 min.

Freezing

We prefer to freeze our berries. They have a better texture after freezing. Wash and dry the berries. Place about ½ pound in a freezer bag trying not to crush the fruit. Narrow the end and using a straw suck out the air from the bag. Seal without letting air re-enter and freeze. The texture is best retained if they are allowed to thaw without heating. No sugar is needed to pack the fruit. You can also place the fruit on trays, in the freezer, to freeze before bagging. This will eliminate clumping of the fruit.

Index

ORDER FORM

Please rush me _____ copies of
FREEDOM FROM ALLERGY
COOKBOOK.
In Canada $16.95 per copy add GST
$1.05 per copy
In U.S.A. $14.95 per copy.

For postage and handling, add
$4.80 for the first and 50¢ for
each additional book.

☐ I can't wait 3-4 weeks for
surface mail. Instead here's $6.00
per copy for Air Mail.

Total enclosed $_____
☐ Cheque   ☐ Money Order
Sorry. credit orders not accepted

Mail order to:
  BLUE POPPY PRESS
  212-2678 West Broadway
  Vancouver, B.C.
  V6K 2G3

Bulk purchase inquiries invited.

Name _____

Address _____

City _____

Prov/State _____

Postal Code/Zip _____

Telephone ( ) _____

ORDER FORM

Please rush me _____ copies of
FREEDOM FROM ALLERGY
COOKBOOK.
 In Canada $16.95 per copy add GST
$1.05 per copy
In U.S.A. $14.95 per copy

For postage and handling, add
$4.80 for the first and 50¢ for
each additional book.

☐ I can't wait 3-4 weeks for
surface mail. Instead here's $6.00
per copy for Air Mail.

Total enclosed $_____
☐ Cheque   ☐ Money Order
Sorry. credit orders not accepted

Mail order to:
  BLUE POPPY PRESS
  212-2678 West Broadway
  Vancouver, B.C.
  V6K 2G3

Bulk purchase inquiries invited.

Name _____

Address _____

City _____

Prov/State _____

Postal Code/Zip _____

Telephone ( ) _____